ART QUILTS INTERNAT

Abstract & Geometric

Martha Sielman

Schiffer Publishing Ltd
4880 Lower Valley Road · Atglen, PA 19310

Designed by Brenda McCallum

Type set in Variable/Goudy Old Style/Agenda

Photographs are courtesy of the artist unless
otherwise noted.

Some portions of the interviews with
Sue Benner, Peggy Brown, Judy Martin, and
Toot Reid were published previously and
are reprinted with permission.

ISBN: 978-0-7643-5220-1

Printed in China

Published by Schiffer Publishing, Ltd.
4880 Lower Valley Road
Atglen, PA 19310
Phone: (610) 593-1777; Fax: (610) 593-2002
E-mail: Info@schifferbooks.com
Web: www.schifferbooks.com

For our complete selection of fine books
on this and related subjects, please visit our
website at www.schifferbooks.com. You may
also write for a free catalog.

Schiffer Publishing's titles are available at
special discounts for bulk purchases for sales
promotions or premiums. Special editions,
including personalized covers, corporate
imprints, and excerpts, can be created in
large quantities for special needs. For more
information, contact the publisher.

We are always looking for people to write
books on new and related subjects. If you have
an idea for a book, please contact us at
proposals@schifferbooks.com.

Other Schiffer Books on Related Subjects:

Fiber Art Today, Carol K. Russell, ISBN 978-0-7643-3777-2

What If Textiles: The Art of Gerhardt Knodel, Contributions by Janet Koplos,
Shelley Selim, Douglas Dawson, Rebecca A. T. Stevens, and Gerhardt Knodel,
ISBN 978-0-7643-4994-2

Japanese Contemporary Quilts and Quilters: The Story of an American Import,
Teresa Duryea Wong, ISBN 978-0-7643-4874-7

Front cover & spine images: Pat Pauly, *Mummy Bags
Influence.* Back cover images, clockwise from top:
Judy Kirpich, *Circles No. 6,* Photo: Mark Gulesian.
Kathleen Loomis, *Entropy,* Photo: George Plager.
Fumiko Nakayama, *Geometric,* Photo: I-jun. Front flap
images, clockwise from top: Anne Solomon,
Welsh Poppies, Photo: Sylvia Galbraith. Linda Frost,
Geode Slices. Yael David-Cohen, *Quartet,*
Photo: Max Alexander. Back flap image: Jean Wells,
High Desert VIII, Photo: Paige Vitek.

Title page image: Uta Lenk, *Play of Lines XXXV:
Shades of Green,* Photo: Andreas Hasak.

Page 3 (Contents) images, L to R: Gay E. Lasher,
Dangerous Curves, Photo: Wes Magyar. Charlotte Bird,
Fruiting Body #9, Photo: Eric Nancarrow.
Judith Larzelere, *Red Volunteer.*

Page 34 images, clockwise from top L: Jeanelle McCall,
Second Blooming. Beth Carney, *Chasms 8,*
Photo: James Dee. Jeanne Marklin, *Going in Circles,*
Photo: Howie Levitz/TGL Photoworks. Marieke
Steenhorst, *Snow on my bedspread (based on a haiku...),*
Photo: M.V. Steenhorst and J. J. Drop. Kate Findlay,
Hidden Universe, Photo: Richard Sedgwick.

Page 100 images, clockwise from top L:
Thelma McGough, *Urban Buzz,* Photo: Roberto
Buzzolan. Judy Kirpich, *Circles No. 6,* Photo: Mark
Gulesian. Helena Scheffer, *Spontaneous Combustion,*
Photo: Maria Korab-Laskowska. Elsbeth Nusser-Lampe,
Spring, Photo: Volker Lampe.

Page 158 images, clockwise from top: Elena Stokes,
Infinity. Jean M. Sredl, *A Time in Stitch.* Cynthia L. Vogt,
Ishi-Datami, Photo: John Warters. Andrea Limmer,
Maelstrom, Photo: Greg Staley.

Page 222 (Index) images, clockwise from top L: Judy
Rush, *Portrait of the Youngest Girl 1.* Sara Impey,
No Exit, Photo: Kevin Mead. Cherry Vernon-Harcourt,
Hunstanton Cliffs. Denyse Schmidt, *Snake Charmer,*
Photo: John Gruen.

Contents

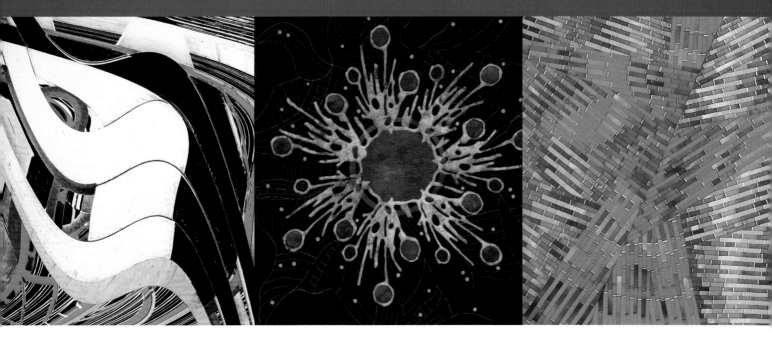

Acknowledgments

A book like this depends on the help of many different people. First of all, I would like to thank my daughter Katie Shaiken, who handled all of the record-keeping to manage details on more than 300 quilts. She also collected all the necessary paperwork, edited the text, reviewed the images, and taught me how to use Google Drive in order to manage all of the information.

I would also like to thank Noriko Endo, who provided invaluable assistance in contacting and communicating with artists in Japan. She has been a continual source of help and advice. Junko Sasaki acted as my translator for the Japanese artists' essays. Her knowledge of the quilt world made those communications go smoothly and successfully.

I extend my thanks to all those who answered the call for entries. Your artwork is inspiring and helped to shape this book. A special thanks to the selected artists for their patience in answering my many questions and for providing the images for this publication.

I would like to thank Nancy and Pete Schiffer for believing in this book and offering me the opportunity to share these wonderful art quilts with the world.

And finally, I would like to thank my husband, David Shaiken, whose love, support, advice, and encouragement gave me the courage to embark on and complete this project. Thank you!

Introduction

I come from a long line of mathematically-inclined ancestors: accountants, doctors, engineers, so it was natural that what first drew me to quilts were the wonderfully symmetrical and richly colored traditional Amish pieces. My own early quilts were all based on simple geometric repetitions, which I found soothing and fun to make.

My sister, Becky Sielman, is an actuary who enjoys hand piecing and hand quilting in the evenings as an antidote to her days at the computer. She made this quilt, *Mathematical Explorations for Charles,* for her son when he went off to college. It explores a variety of mathematical puzzles, fractal designs, and complex tetrahedrons. Mathematical symbols are quilted into the border. Family background thus pulls me toward geometrical designs, a special category of abstract art quilts.

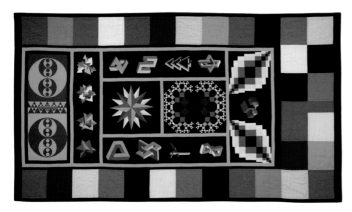

BECKY SIELMAN. *Mathematical Explorations for Charles.* 2014. 55" × 99". Commercial fabrics. Hand appliquéd, hand quilted. Photo: Deidre Adams.

As executive director of Studio Art Quilt Associates, Inc. (SAQA), I'm involved each year in putting together an annual portfolio of work by SAQA's Juried Artist Members. Each year about half of the images we receive are abstract art quilts, so when I began to put together this volume of my series on art quilts I knew that I would have a wealth of images to draw upon. However, I was overwhelmed by the response to my call for entries. I received more than 1,300 submissions from 461 artists! This made choosing the artists and images to feature in this book very challenging, as I could have written several books with all the wonderful art that I received.

In the end, I chose these 97 gallery and 29 featured artists based on a variety of factors. Most importantly, their work stuck in my head. I kept coming back to these powerful images that grabbed my attention and wouldn't let go. I also looked for a variety of approaches to abstract and geometric work. The imagery in this book varies from completely non-representational explorations of color and form, to abstracted realistic imagery, to the ultimate in abstraction—words: symbols that stand for concepts and emotions.

I also wanted to celebrate the global nature of the art quilt community, and I am delighted to be able to share work by artists from eighteen countries: Australia, Canada, France, Germany, Israel, Italy, Japan, Latvia, the Netherlands, Northern Ireland, Russia, South Africa, Spain, Sweden, Switzerland, Taiwan, the UK, and across the US. Though they live in many different places, they all share a passion for working with fabric and thread. It has been a pleasure to get to know these artists from around the world.

I interviewed each of the featured artists about their inspirations, their working methods, and their challenges. Each artist has a different story to tell. I enjoyed learning about Deidre Adams's discovery of discarded textbooks, whose pages she incorporates into her painted imagery. Denyse Schmidt has revolutionized the quilt world by bringing a modern design aesthetic to traditional patterns.

Fumiko Nakayama first discovered the mola style of reverse appliqué in 1967. She says that seeing that first mola was like experiencing an electric shock, and she has gone on to develop an incredible body of work of her own design, as well as teaching her approach to hundreds of students in Japan. Sue Benner's early degree in molecular biology has influenced her design aesthetic, so her circles represent cells with nuclei and cytoplasm, while her childhood in Wisconsin wearing and sewing her own plaid skirts has instilled a fascination with how lines intersect.

And those are only four of the selected feature artists. I know that you will enjoy learning more about each of the artists. Together we worked to choose an array of their work that best showcases their talents. It has been a real privilege for me to be offered this glimpse into their lives and creative process.

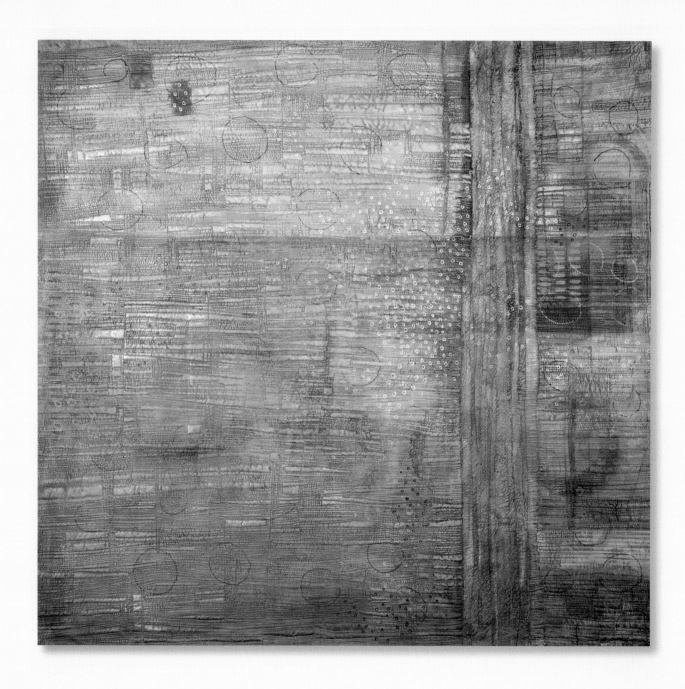

Deidre Adams

Littleton, Colorado, USA

A recurring theme in Deidre Adams's art is experimentation. Earlier work pioneered a technique of painting over a quilted surface to create exciting visual texture. Her more recent series uses reclaimed papers to metaphorically and literally peel back layers of meaning.

Photography creates focus

The act of photography concentrates my focus into specific areas of observation. I like to look at the world through the camera's viewfinder, zooming in closely and eliminating recognizable details. This allows an abstraction of structure and surface into new, singular compositions. I'm also attracted to surfaces that bear the marks of time and transformation. Although I don't create literal representations of these photographs in my paintings, I've internalized their appearance and character to the extent that their presence in my mind affects everything I do.

Paint over stitch

When I discovered that I could use paint to emphasize my stitching, it became a primary technique in my work. I simplified the construction of the piece's top layer, choosing fabrics at random, with an eye toward how the pattern and color would create underlying visual texture as the base of my layering process. This freed me to concentrate more on the process of the quilting, and I started doing more and more stitching.

The quilting designs are never planned in advance, though I do have a repertoire of patterns that I use over and over again. I use the underlying seams from the piecing as a sort of guide to where I'll break from one pattern to another, but it's pretty loose. I listen to music while I'm working to prevent me from thinking too much about what my hands are doing.

Writing

One of my past artistic endeavors was learning calligraphy. I've always been attracted to letterforms and ideograms from all languages, whether beautifully executed as in ancient texts or hurriedly scribbled on a wall or in the street. In some cases the intent is only to impart a message to those who know the code, and sometimes that's combined with a desire to create something beautiful and lasting.

Incorporating writing into my textile work started around the time I received a commission for a small neighborhood library. In this series, called *Chronicles,* I wanted to impart the idea of communication and learning, so I started writing on the pieces. It's stream-of-consciousness writing, but my brain goes much faster than my hand, so letters and full words are dropped out, it's messy, and it can't be read by anybody.

OPPOSITE *Composition IX.* 2008. 46" × 48".
Commercial fabrics, acrylic paint. Machine stitched, hand painted.

Returning to the Source. 2012. 78" × 32".
Commercial fabrics, acrylic paint. Machine stitched, hand painted.

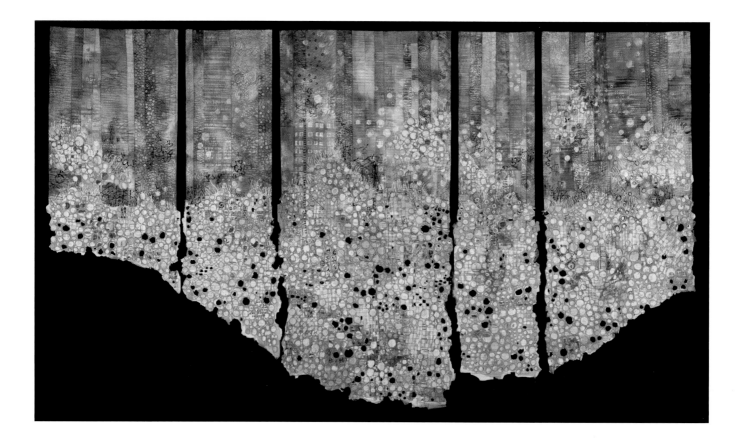

Adding paper

I have a collection of various vintage textbooks that I've picked up from free bins, as well as maps and sheet music and other things that I thought I might use for collage work. I began by simply experimenting with stitching onto layered sheets, and then I got the idea to start peeling them back to reveal what was underneath.

This process is informed and reinforced by my attraction to the history of a place and to structures that have been abandoned, weathered by time and the elements. The paper is also a stand-in for an abstract idea of the collective knowledge of all human beings throughout time and our efforts to make sense of the world and communicate it to others.

As I work on these, I've started to picture them from the point of view of a sort of archaeologist from the future, perhaps from a faraway planet, who comes to Earth after we've destroyed our society and tries to make sense of all the many and varied materials we left behind, perhaps in an attempt to learn what happened to us. I'm thinking about the incredible amount of knowledge and information available in the world, but at the same time how it is not available to everyone.

TOP *Disruption*. 2014. 55" × 98".
Commercial fabrics, acrylic paint, paper from various sources: dictionaries, textbooks, maps, sheet music, novels, and other found materials. Machine stitched, hand painted; layered papers peeled and torn.

BOTTOM *Composition VI*. 2008. 36" × 36".
Commercial fabrics, acrylic paint. Machine stitched, hand painted.

I'm inspired by a lot of things: my photos of old walls with flaking stuff and layers revealed, old floors, maps. Not only that, but the evolution of things in a news story; the cycle in which day by day the layers are peeled back and more is revealed, showing that there is always more to a thing than meets the eye. I always love a process that involves both creation and destruction, building up and tearing down.

Roller coaster of emotion

Every piece involves a roller coaster of emotion—on the one hand, total happiness and well-being during the process of making. On the other hand, fear and despair over how things are coming out. I'm no longer surprised at this; it's as familiar as an old friend. The key is to keep going, no matter what.

ABOVE *Tracings VIII*. 2014. 60" × 22". Commercial fabrics, acrylic paint, paper from various sources: dictionaries, textbooks, maps, sheet music, novels, and other found materials. Machine stitched, hand painted; layered papers peeled and torn.

LEFT *Tracings VII*. 2014. 60" × 22". Commercial fabrics, acrylic paint, paper from various sources: dictionaries, textbooks, maps, sheet music, novels, and other found materials. Machine stitched, hand painted; layered papers peeled and torn.

Daphne Taylor

Montville, Maine, USA

Monochromatic fields of silk are shaped by gestural stitched marks in Daphne Taylor's work. An interplay of light and shadow is created by subtle changes in the stitched lines. Each meditative stitch serves a particular purpose: nothing should be added or taken away.

Simplicity

My Quaker roots gave me a deep appreciation for the power of silence and simplicity. In my childhood, these common practices were part of a way of life for which I am grateful. To me, the practice of simplicity strips away excess, metaphorically, literally, and leaves one with the essence and the necessary.

There is a lot of overlap between a spiritual practice of sitting in silence with nothing but your breath, and one's art practice. In both, it is a practice of stripping away: one to the breath; the other to a world of appreciative wonderment that is always there to be looked at, studied, and expressed in the simplest visual language possible.

Drawing

What fascinates me about the lines and forms that recur in my quilts comes from a lifelong love of drawing. Drawing has always been an intuitive, natural act for me—a second language, often more accessible than speaking or writing. It is at the core of all my work.

The use of line in all my quilts honors my love of that spontaneous marking often found in quick drawings. I honor the marks of my particular hand. How to incorporate it into the quilting is an ongoing exploration of design, movement, and restraint.

Recently I have become interested in the transitions of my quilted fields into the space around them. I know it adds a particular vitality. While I love playing with letting the line extend out beyond the formal shape, I am cautious to not let this design element become predictable and safe.

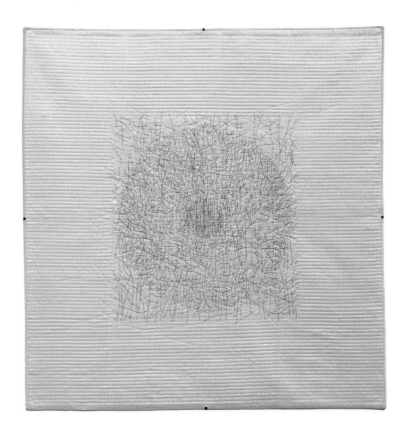

OPPOSITE *Quilt Drawing #12*. 2009. 29" × 30". Silk fabric, cotton poly thread. Whole cloth, hand quilted, hand embroidered. | Photo: Karen Bell.

TOP *Quilt Drawing #16*. 2012. 51" × 50". Silk fabric, cotton poly thread. Whole cloth, hand quilted, hand embroidered. | Photo: James Dee.

BOTTOM *Quilt Drawing #18*. 2014. 41" × 41". Silk fabric, cotton poly thread. Machine pieced, hand embroidered, hand quilted. | Photo: Jean Vong.

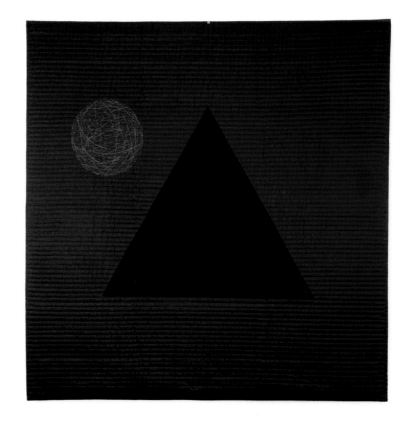

White silk

Silk is a painter's cloth. The silks have a surface and luminosity that create different color experiences under different light conditions. A vast field of off-white silk is a stunning surface to have the eye graze over. This is where I have often begun with my work, envisioning the progression of adding various quilted shadow lines into this sea of white silk. I could work with white silk for the rest of my life, as the beauty of light and shadow is ever present and abundant with possibility.

I am slowly beginning to work with color again. However, I am cautious as I find it difficult to create a piece that goes beyond being a beautifully designed quilt on the wall. I tell people that if I knew what to do with color, I would. And some day I hope to.

All of my quilts are hand quilted. Hand quilting is essential to me because it gives the fabric surface the mark of the hand, a human presence that cannot easily be achieved by machine. The process slows one down and teaches one much about being in the moment with each thread and stitch, easily redoing each part until it is right but never knowing what the final visual presence will be. Hand quilting is its own meditation, which I value. It gives me the time to think about my work in a different way—slowly pulling out an image that takes months to achieve.

Quilt Drawing #13: For Maureen. 2010. 46" × 39". Silk fabric, cotton poly thread. Whole cloth, hand quilted, hand embroidered. Photo: James Dee.

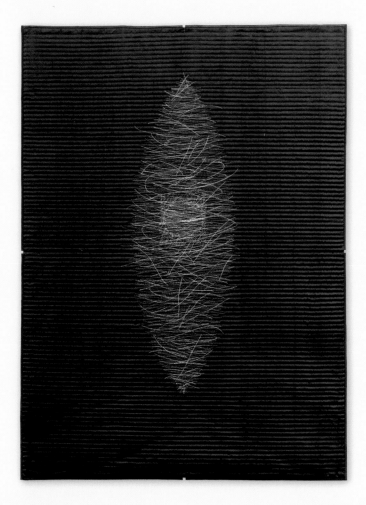

Imagery

My quilts are fueled by a deep desire to create works that inspire awe and encourage the viewer to experience a quiet presence. My imagery often starts out of a wish to honor the formal design relationships of basic shapes: the circle, the square, and the triangle. If one strips away representation this is what you will find, and it is here I began and still am.

None of my work is preplanned. I have a vision or aura that I am curious to pursue. In each new quilt, there is often some technical element that I am exploring to expand my visual vocabulary of line, shading, and shadow. Each piece takes close to a year to complete. With almost every quilt, around four to five months into the quilting, I ask myself, "What am I doing? What's going on here? Nothing is working." I have come to value this moment as the moment when the true work of what I am going after is being challenged for clarity, and I rise to answer it.

This is where I am. It is a slow, contemplative process that the hand quilting supports. And thus my work evolves slowly.

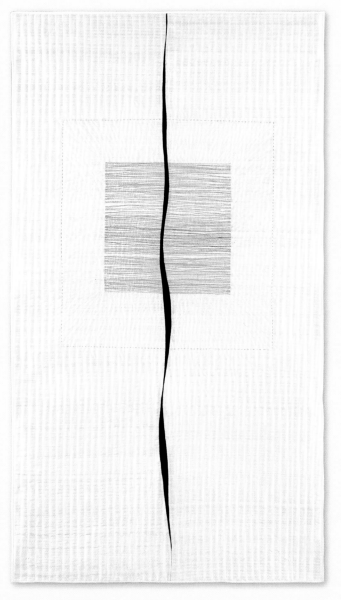

LEFT *Quilt Drawing #15*. 2012. 53" × 39".
Silk fabric, cotton poly and metallic threads. Whole cloth, hand quilted, hand embroidered. | Photo: James Dee.

RIGHT *Quilt Drawing #9*. 2009. 50" × 25".
Silk, cotton fabrics, cotton embroidery thread. Machine pieced, hand quilted, hand embroidered. | Photo: Karen Bell.

Kathy Weaver

Highland Park, Illinois, USA

Exploration of an alternative world, a microcosmic mixture of organic and mechanistic forms characterizes Kathy Weaver's work. Combining airbrushed compositions and hand-stitched details further highlights the contrast of natural and robotic. Views of these possible futuristic developments both attract and repulse, part of the phenomenon where we tend to reject anything that is too human-like but not actually human.

My parents

I grew up with a father who was involved in the manufacturing of electronic components for television and radio. Progress and the concurrent speed of development of new products were always a topic of conversation in our house. My father was very much a futurist. With a partner he manufactured the first white noise machines. Ahead of their time, our garage was a warehouse for hundreds of "Sound Sleepers."

Quilting creates a link to my mother, my grandmother, and her sisters, all of whom were wonderful needleworkers. I have fond memories of stitching beside them on long afternoons in their sunroom sewing porches. Cloth brings forth myriad reactions and associations. Using cloth allows me to bring layers of meaning to my work, which references our bodies, childhood, gender, and our own mortality.

Robots and nano views

Almost fifteen years ago, I started exploring robots as subject matter in my art. I wanted to question the status quo, examine the environment, and challenge the industrial-military complex. In 2006 I attended a world conference on artificial information and robotics at Indiana University. This experience informed my work about robotics as a field of study and research and led to my investigation of the military's use of robots. In addition, for the past several years I have been drawing at the Robotics Department at the Rehabilitation Institute of Chicago, where I have observed scientists making prototypes of robots that help patients with traumatic injuries.

The airbrushed and embroidered *Life Form* series and the larger organic pieces, such as *Generated Topology* and *Strategic Alliance*, evoke an alternative world where details are shown on a macro scale. The forms use artificial intelligence as source material and draw from photographic and microscope scans of simple-celled plants and animals. These species represent the life source, the spark in the primordial soup from which we evolved. I use bird's-eye view, multiple levels, and large forms to explore the environment from the robot's point of view, to see the interiors of an unearthly, intriguing, and threatening world.

OPPOSITE *Crude Explorations*. 2010. 51" × 55".
Satin. Airbrushed, hand quilted. | Photo: Tom Van Eynde.

Fragile Vibrations. 2010. 63" × 31".
Satin. Airbrushed, hand embroidered, hand quilted. | Photo: Tom Van Eynde.

Airbrushing and hand quilting

I originally decided on an airbrush as a tool because I wanted the robots to look mechanistic. I did not want the artist's hand to be a part of the composition. I took a course at a local junior college with students who were learning to do taxidermy and to paint motorcycles, trucks, and shirts using airbrushing.

I create my pieces by airbrushing and sewing what is in my subconscious without preliminary sketches or plans. I start with a blank piece of bridal satin and then use the airbrush and tape to lay out a structure, moving around the picture plane quickly and rhythmically. I then try to read my own thoughts as they are shown on the satin, creating more intersections and forms as I progress. The details are done using various stencils I have made or found, layering them as I build up areas of dark and light. The paint I use is transparent so layers are built up as the piece progresses toward completion.

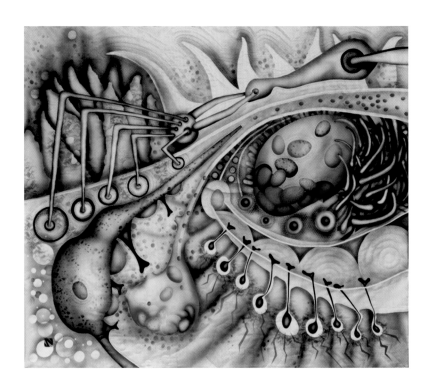

In contrast, the meditative aspect of hand quilting is really appealing to me. I also know that people appreciate the element of time an artist spends doing hand quilting. This time passage is subconsciously "read" by the viewer and adds weight to the importance or intent of the piece. In addition, I like the contrast of hand quilting a technologically advanced life-form or robot.

ABOVE *Strategic Alliance*. 2008. 48" × 55". Satin. Airbrushed, hand quilted. Photo: Tom Van Eynde.

LEFT *Generated Topology*. 2008. 42" × 48". Satin. Airbrushed, hand quilted. Photo: Tom Van Eynde.

Art as a reflector of the world

Currently I am doing a series called *Collateral Damage*, which has to do with the effects of war on the environment and the civilian population. I enjoy the research that goes into these kinds of topical works. I like being engaged and informed about other places and situations in the world. I see doing this kind of work as my political contribution. I can use my talents to hopefully engage others to think about the state of our country and the world. I attempt to create these feelings in my work by being colorful, humorous, ironic, wry, and truthful.

I see the world as a complex, fascinating, layered place. Surprises are everywhere, and things are often not as they appear. Humor and pathos share equal space, sometimes in the same place, moment, or person. Duality and the juxtaposition of opposites play an important role in both how I see the world and how I depict it in my work.

ABOVE *Correlated Pathways*. 2009. 50" × 50". Canvas. Airbrushed, hand quilted. Photo: Tom Van Eynde.

LEFT *Optimized Persistence*. 2009. 36" × 36". Satin. Airbrushed, hand embroidered, hand quilted. | Photo: Tom Van Eynde.

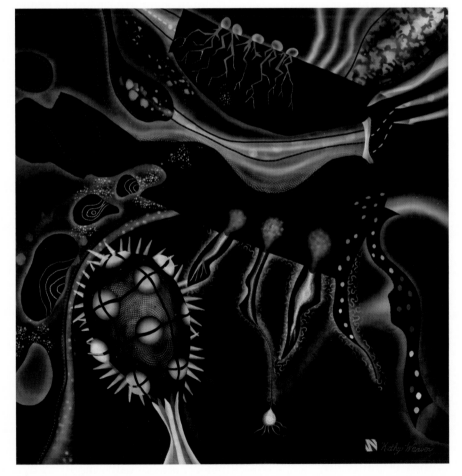

Gay E. Lasher
Denver, Colorado, USA

An enduring fascination with construction sites shapes Gay E. Lasher's work. She has been taking photographs of construction detritus for over thirty years. Her art expands the basic lines and shapes of her photos into wonderfully abstract compositions in which the original objects are just barely discernible and the colors vibrate in a way no construction site ever has.

Many artistic paths

In the late 1960s, I began to explore weaving. I had knitted for many years and weaving was another way of putting threads together to make cloth. Eventually I became frustrated with the loom set-up process and moved on briefly to batik, making small dolls. As I worked on the dolls, I realized that my drawing skills were quite limited and decided to take a drawing class at Metropolitan State University of Denver. One drawing class led to three semesters of drawing and then to three years of undergraduate art classes, resulting in a degree in fine art.

Deciding to get a fine art education was probably the most important decision I ever made. I cannot stress enough just how important this was. The classes gave me the vocabulary with which to talk about art, greatly improved my skills, exposed me to different media, and expanded my horizons. I also took an introductory photography class and totally fell in love.

OPPOSITE *No Turn on Red.* 2014. 31" × 41". Paper-backed cotton sheeting, archival inks. Computer-altered photographic elements printed on cotton, pieced panels, machine quilted. Photo: Wes Magyar.

ABOVE *In the Beginning.* 2012. 52" × 46". Paper-backed cotton sheeting, archival inks, acrylic inks, hemming tape. Computer-altered photographic elements printed on cotton, pieced panels, machine quilted, trapunto. | Photo: Deidre Adams.

RIGHT *First Moment.* 2013. 48" × 46". Paper-backed cotton sheeting, archival inks. Computer-altered photographic elements printed on cotton, pieced panels, machine quilted. Photo: Deidre Adams.

Crash Zone. 2014. 28" × 40". Paper-backed cotton sheeting, archival inks. Computer-altered photographic elements printed on cotton, pieced panels, machine quilted. | Photo: Wes Magyar.

Photoshop discovery

After my retirement from a career in psychology in 2003, I wanted to return to textiles and decided to try art quilts. It seemed natural to combine digital photography with the work that I was doing. When I first started experimenting with my photographs in Adobe Photoshop, I began by changing the color saturation, but the altered image was not appealing to me. It still looked too much like what it had originally been.

When I began playing with the filters, the first one I tried was called artistic cutout. When that filter is applied, the resulting image appears on the monitor at a size which is larger than can be displayed on the monitor. Only a section appears at any one time and to see other areas you have to scroll. I could therefore only see a portion of the whole image, and because it was a small portion it became abstracted. I was very excited because I could see the possibilities for creating other abstractions from my photographs of local sites, particularly construction sites.

Follow the black thread

Once an image is printed, the panels are sewn together, and the quilt sandwich is made, I start to think about how I will quilt the piece. I don't have any preconceived quilting plan, except to start in the center and work my way outwards.

I usually choose a particular starting point and use black thread to outline areas. As I go along, the thread often knows where it wants to go, whether in a straight line or around a curve or creating a tiny detail highlighting a particular shape. I almost always quilt at half-speed so I can accommodate these on-the-spot decisions. Over time, I have learned that if a shape needs to have some stitching with different colors inside it, to do that stitching before enclosing the area with black thread to avoid puckering on the back of the quilt.

Limitless edges

With the abstractions, I am extracting a small detail from an entire photograph composition. A slightly different choice of area would create a very different piece if I had framed it on the computer just a little to the left, right, top, or bottom. The image I choose is just one of a myriad possible images.

I don't want the edges to be pinned down and enclosed by a border. Without borders, the viewer is free to imagine the piece continuing in all directions.

Playing in Traffic series

My husband and I go at least once a week to the Cherry Creek area in Denver, which has a relatively small and concentrated business area and a major intersection. Starting a few years ago, it seemed that each week when we arrived there, another gigantic hole was in the ground, hard hats were everywhere, and construction trucks and heavy machinery of all kinds were taking over. Encountering this mess became our weekly experience.

I had made a piece titled *Dangerous Curves*. The thought occurred to me to extend that idea into a series of abstract images about traffic. I decided to try to keep the color palette of all the work in this series as consistent as possible and to use images extracted from just two basic photographs to keep the elements in the compositions fairly consistent. I wanted to communicate the frenzy and frustration of my traffic experiences. Working to a theme with a consistent color palette has been an interesting and stimulating challenge.

ABOVE *Abstraction IV.* 2010. 46" × 33". Paper-backed cotton sheeting, archival inks. Computer-altered photographic elements printed on cotton, pieced panels, machine quilted. | Photo: Deidre Adams.

LEFT *Dangerous Curves.* 2014. 49" × 46". Paper-backed cotton sheeting, archival inks. Computer-altered photographic elements printed on cotton, pieced panels, machine quilted. | Photo: Wes Magyar.

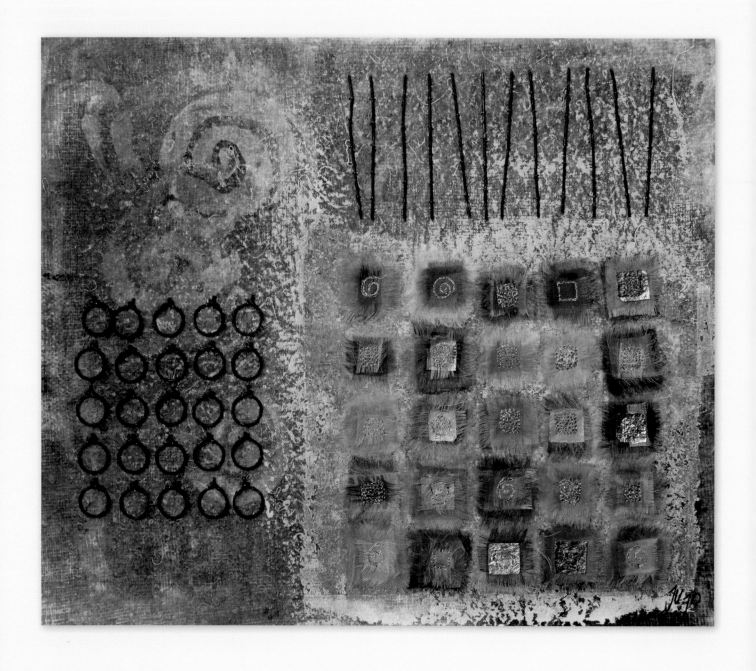

Judith Mundwiler

Buus, Switzerland

An amazing array of materials find their way into Judith Mundwiler's work: metals, papers, seed pods, tea bags. Colors range from subtle neutral tones to wildly vibrant silken sheens and shimmering gold foils. This wild abundance is tamed into orderly grids, sensually soothing in their regularity and repetition.

Recycled materials

You will find almost no new materials in my work. I'm interested in the history of an object that had a purpose, such as wrapping paper, or aluminum foil from a chocolate, or a page from an old book. When I hold this material in my hands, I always ask the question: "What can I do with this before I discard it in the trash?" I like to give these materials a new life.

In my colored quilts, I use Korean silk organza that I get as remnants from a Korean tailoring firm in Los Angeles. This material fascinates me because of the enormous brightness of the colors and because of its transparency. I especially like to combine this soft fabric with cold, hard metal. The color of the metal, especially of rusted metal, works well against the colored silk. I collect metal found objects during my walks in the street. I also often use gold foil from chocolates. The metal film shimmers and shines beautifully.

In one of my series, I sewed exclusively with used tea bags, which friends gathered for me. I experimented with this fascinating material and examined ways in which I could paint these fragile pieces of paper, embroider, and laminate them so that I could sew them together without destroying the wonderful essence of tea.

OPPOSITE *Daily Treasures*. 2010. 12" × 16".
Felt, Korean silk, foil from chocolates, copper wire.
Screen printed, hand and machine stitched.

TOP *Dance of the Flowers*. 2007. 30" × 19".
Plants and grasses. Sewn by machine.

BOTTOM *My Mysterious Garden*. 2010. 39" × 39".
Children's drawings on paper, chiffon.
Machine embroidered.

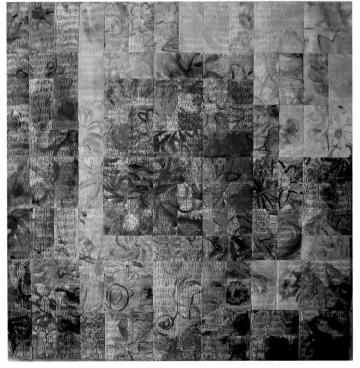

Grids and frayed edges

Grids help me to bring order into my thoughts. It is a kind of meditation. I create individual, small stories, each of which has something to tell. The grid brings together many of these little stories into a larger narrative. The squares in the grids create beautiful color transitions, each one becoming a color pixel.

When I made my first quilt forty years ago using a paper piecing technique, I realized that the straight, clean edges bothered me. I felt that they limited my expression. My first training was as a dressmaker, so I know how to sew very exactly, but my second job was as a school teacher and I learned from the children that a crookedly cut fabric or a frayed edge creates a much greater sense of ease and freedom.

That is why I work with frayed edges on my fabrics. The fraying creates a fringe, which appears light and airy. The color transitions are wonderful. If this Korean silk were cut into perfect squares, the whole effect would be lost.

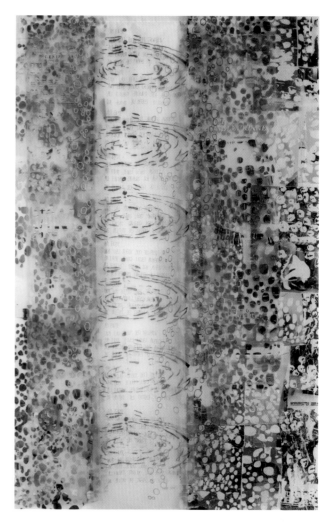

Inspiration from nature

I am inspired by nature, and I often photograph it. However, I do not use my photographs directly for ideas for my work. In my book *Textile Treasures*, which combined my photographs with my textile art, I was trying to show that the way that I perceive my surroundings, my environment, is similar to what I try to express in my quilts. I do not draw in a sketchbook, but I do have a journal where I write down ideas.

ABOVE *In the end.* 2009. 55" × 31".
Organza, chiffon, paper. Paper lamination on fabric.
Machine sewn, machine embroidered, layered.

LEFT *Teatime in the Evening.* 2014. 47" × 31".
Fabrics, papers, used tea bags. Hand embroidered.

Use of text

In *My Mysterious Garden*, each word describes that portion of the piece. In each rectangle I have repeated the name of the flowers: poppy, lily, marguerite, or I have written "water" or "shadow." This type of writing is very literal, but for *In the End*, I interpreted a poem from my friend Susanne Ernst.

Susanne wrote the poem and I interpreted its meaning in fabric, but the poem is also written out as a component in the white middle part of the piece. I have written it several times on the organza. The poem is about the drop of water that finds its way. Therefore, the color is blue and I have printed water drops on the fabric and embroidered them as well. The images in the background are from my journals reflecting on the topics of impermanence and the aging process. If you look closely at the photo right on the edge, about in the middle, you will see an elderly couple hugging each other tenderly.

Medicago aurum. 2009. 29" × 28". Korean silk, aluminum foils from chocolates. Hand sewn.

Peggy Brown

Nashville, Indiana, USA

Delicate watercolors in Peggy Brown's art combine organic forms created by the chance movement of pigment with the deliberate placement of ordered rows of small squares marching across the surface. Quilted lines run busily back and forth, emphasizing some areas and blending others together. Like a mysterious map, they are signposts to the artist's lifelong fascination with color and paint.

Collaboration with the medium

My art is a collaboration between watercolor, the medium, and myself, the artist. I think we both enjoy ourselves. I emphasize the "water" part of watercolor, because I work extremely wet so the pigments follow their own designs: some granulate and make textures, others stain, others mix and form beautiful sensitive colors. It takes time and experience for a painter to learn to let watercolor be watercolor. I let the medium do its own thing, and then I take over and finish things up. I feel we work well together.

Painting on paper and fabric

I paint on both paper and fabric. I use the same media (transparent watercolor), tools, and methods for both. To begin the process I place the substrate on a waterproof surface. Then I wet the paper or fabric with water from a sponge or a spray bottle and freely brush on paint allowing the pigments to mingle and follow their personal paths. As the paint dries, shapes and colors begin to emerge that I could never totally plan or predict. During this initial step I let the medium with its impetuous yet sensitive manner be my guide, while I assert only semi-control.

Usually I repeat the first step several times to add more texture, depth, and richness. During

OPPOSITE *Three Times Three.* 2014. 43" × 53".
Silk habotai, silk organza, digital transfers from artist's paintings, transparent watercolor paint. Hand painted, digital transfer, collaged, fused, machine quilted.

TOP *Tulips and Trees.* 2014. 40" × 39".
Silk habotai folded and painted with transparent watercolor, papers with digital transfers from artist's drawings and paintings, paint. Hand painted, collaged, digital transfer, fused, machine quilted.

BOTTOM *Landscape/Sunrise Sunset.* 2013. 39" × 36".
Silk, archival tissue, transparent watercolor paint. Painted, collaged, fused, machine quilted.

the second part of the journey I look over the painted base and let the surface design inspire me. Since the wet paint flows through the fabric, the textures can be more interesting on the reverse side and often the back becomes my new front. Following the suggested imagery on the painted substrate, I begin laying out several different designs using painted and transferred fabrics and papers from my stash. When I'm happy with the design I fuse the collage to the background and tie everything together with more painting, collage, and drawing. My goal is to take a free-flowing start and using collage with overlays of more pigment and drawing, compose a well-designed finish.

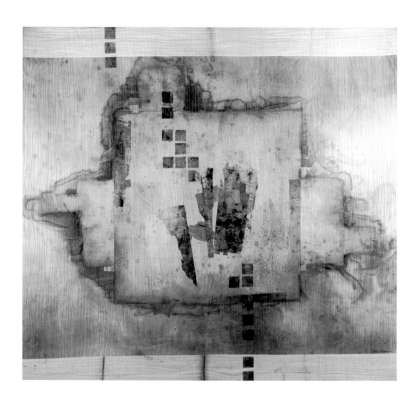

TOP *Moments.* 2014. 43" × 40".
Silk, archival tissue, digital transfers from artist's paintings, transparent watercolor paint. Painted, digital transfer, collaged, fused, machine quilted.

BOTTOM *Blue in the Abstract.* 2013. 44" × 40".
Silk, interfacing, archival tissue, digital transfers of artist's painting transparent watercolor paint. Painted, digital transfer, collaged, fused, machine quilted.

Shades of Italy III. 2011. 41" × 31".
Flannel, archival tissue, digital
transfers of artist's paintings,
transparent watercolor paint.
Painted, digital transfer, collaged,
fused, machine quilted.
Photo: Chandon Photographers.

Moments

An example is *Moments*, which began with a digital transfer
to tissue paper. The image of the transfer was of a section
of one of my paintings on paper. I coated the transfer
with acrylic. When it was dry, I tore the paper into angled
sections, rearranged their order and mounted them onto
a previously painted square piece of cotton. Next I painted
a large piece of silk with colors to complement the center.
I tore some unpainted tissue paper into geometric forms,
painted, arranged, and fused them, along with the central
square piece, onto the painted silk. After repainting and
brushing acrylic matte medium over the paper sections,
I painted around and over the edges of the collage with grey
to unite all sections. Softly painted silk borders on the top
and bottom, and collaged little squares that lead the eye
through the image, completed my design.

Transparency

My geometric shapes are abstracted from my old paintings
of Victorian houses, barns, etc. Tree branches inspire the
organic lines that flow through most of my work. I like the
juxtaposition of the geometric forms with the organic lines
and the fact that the geometric shapes anchor the design
while the organic lines unite it.

I try to express images that appear on, above, and below
the surface. I do this by keeping all layers transparent with
the use of transparent paint, transparent papers, and at times
transparent fabrics such as organza and interfacing. I invite
the viewer to follow as I work and see through the topmost
layer, through the intermediate layers, to the substrate with
its beginning of the design.

Harue Konishi

Tokyo, Japan

A continuous drive to explore infuses the designs of Harue Konishi's art. Working with the purest of lines, shapes, and colors, she constantly experiments with how differences in the weight of a line, sparks of color, or a focus on the threads will change the feel of a piece. While good design may be simple, achieving true simplicity is no easy task.

Beginnings

I was about ten years old when I began sewing by making things like dresses for my dolls. My mother guided me. I became interested in quilts thirty-five years ago. There were many Japanese kimono in my house, and I wanted to do something with them. My love for fabrics prompted me to take on quilting.

Inspiration from fabric

Fabrics are the source of inspiration for all my works. It always starts with fabric. Japanese kimono fabrics are very individualistic and often have intricate embroidery. I pieced and quilted by hand in my early work, but recent works are all done by machine.

In *SYO #74*, the fine lines are all pieced. For other pieces, I have created thin lines using satin stitch, but I felt it would be negligent of me to do so for this piece. Because this is a patchwork quilt, I wanted to stick to piecing.

The fabrics used for the color highlights are made from meisen fabrics with red and green dots on a black background. I cut the silk into tiny strips and pieced them into the white fabric, so that the color would assert itself in a modest way.

With *SYO #58*, I wanted to challenge my skills and see how I could create an entire piece of thin lines. I thought again of using satin stitch, but something in me did not allow myself to take the same approach. I had to try to execute it with piecing. There is lots of room to develop this design method that is continually challenging.

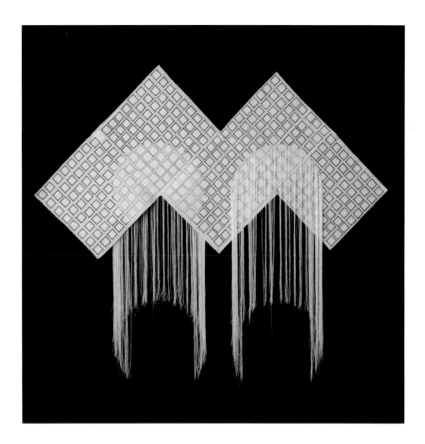

OPPOSITE *SYO #74*. 2014. 55" × 58".
Silk. Machine pieced, machine quilted.

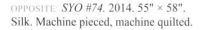

TOP *SYO #32*. 2009. 53" × 47".
Silk. Machine pieced, machine quilted.

BOTTOM *SYO #39*. 2010. 53" × 47".
Silk. Machine pieced, machine quilted.

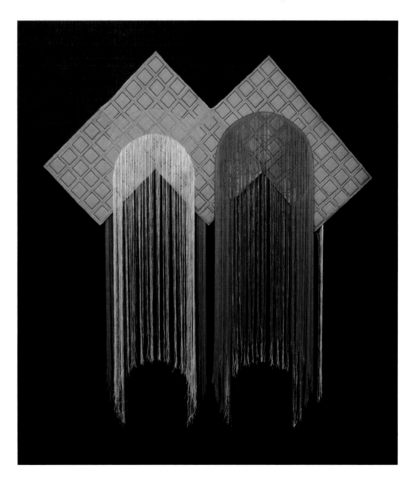

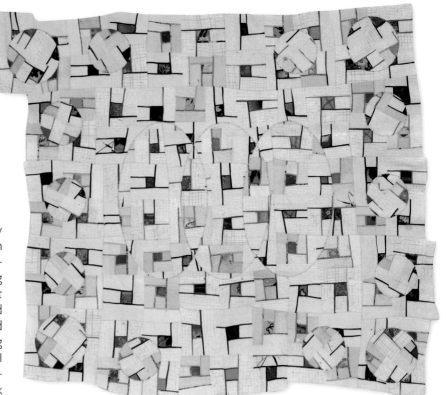

Loose threads

SYO #32 contains circular designs formed by a pattern of long threads. Other pieces in the series have long, loose threads throughout the design. I've experimented with using short, loose threads as an intentional part of design, but many people misunderstood what I was attempting and thought they had not been properly finished. I enjoyed making these works, but it got to the point where I found it difficult to evolve the designs further, and therefore I needed to take a break from it.

Magnification

Recent quilts, such as *SYO #66*, have sections that contain designs that are subtly different from the background. The effect is like looking through a magnifying lens. What I find satisfying is to create a subtle difference that at a glance looks similar, but when you look closely you notice something different.

This square pattern is my current favorite. I can make it look fun or bold by changing the size of the center square, or make it look cute by changing the color to red or green. I've also been experimenting with irregularly shaped quilts. I think in rectangles at the design stage, but sometimes they morph as the production progresses. I do prefer rectangles to circles.

TOP *SYO #66.* 2012. 69" × 53".
Silk. Machine pieced, machine quilted.

BOTTOM *SYO #69.* 2013. 39" × 53".
Silk. Machine pieced, machine quilted.

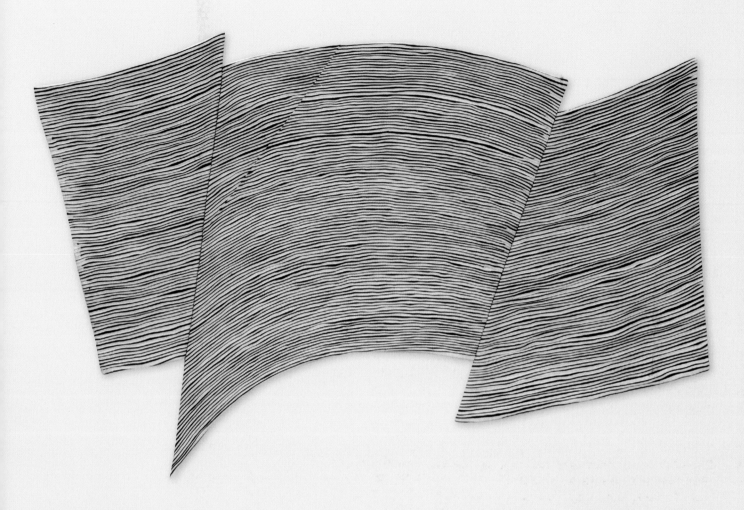

Minimalist designs

In *SYO #69*, the design is extremely simplified in black on white with just two patches of colored fabric for accents. The squares are indicated by just two sides and the off-set shapes are also square.

I make all my works using Japanese kimono fabrics. The old kimono fabrics have such strong individuality that they are not easy materials to handle. For this work I used white oshima silk and chirimen navy blue striped silk. My recent works, including this one, employ a process where I finish the whole thing in the first stage and then rotate shapes by cutting them out, changing their angles, and embedding them back into the original piece.

Have you seen the kind of photographic art that uses mirrors in a prairie? The mirrors reflect similar prairie views, but they create another space. It is as though it exists and does not exist at the same time. That's the idea I am trying to pursue in my quilts. It is the same but not the same.

Good design is simple

Good design to me means simple. It is very important that it look simple despite the fact that it has gone through a complicated creative process. Good design also means that the shapes express my senses, my feelings. To me, design should not be obscure. The simpler it is, the more that the design really clicks with me.

Although some designs come quickly, it generally takes time to develop a design. I become very preoccupied when I am in the middle of the design process. However, the ones that come to me quickly tend to be more satisfactory.

SYO #58. 2012. 55" × 36". Silk. Machine pieced, machine quilted.

Rosemary Hoffenberg

Massachusetts, USA.
Three Musicians. 2013. 45" × 34".
Cotton. Dyed, painted, screen printed, machine pieced,
machine appliquéd, machine quilted. | Photo: Joe Ofria.

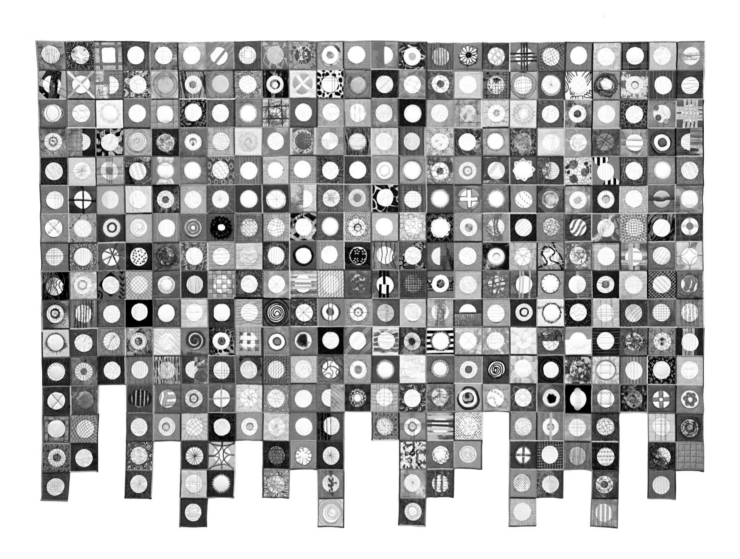

Cécile Trentini

Zurich, Switzerland.
Daily Beauty. 2010. 66" × 93".
Cotton, polyester, silk, linen, organza, netting, cheesecloth, make-up sponges,
plastics, sequins, beads, buttons, lace, ribbons, found objects. Sewn, quilted,
embroidered, printed, fused. | Photo: C&T Publishing.

Marina Kamenskaya

Illinois, USA.
Edge #6. 2009. 69" × 69".
Cotton. Pieced, quilted.

Jae McDonald

Oregon, USA.
Red Center. 2007. 35" × 52".
Cotton, dupioni silk. Machine pieced and quilted,
hand embroidered. | Photo: Jon Christopher Meyers.

Jeanelle McCall

Texas, USA.
Second Blooming. 2013. 26" × 37".
Cotton, linen, silk, lace, polyester.
Free motion embroidered, hand stitched.

Elizabeth Barton
Georgia, USA.
Black and White, *No Grey*. 2009. 53" × 38".
Cotton. Pieced, hand and machine quilted.
Photo: Karen Hamrick.

Irene MacWilliam

Belfast, Northern Ireland.
9 Patch Illusion. 2010. 35" × 34".
Cotton. Raw edge appliqué, machine quilted.
Photo: Susan MacWilliam.

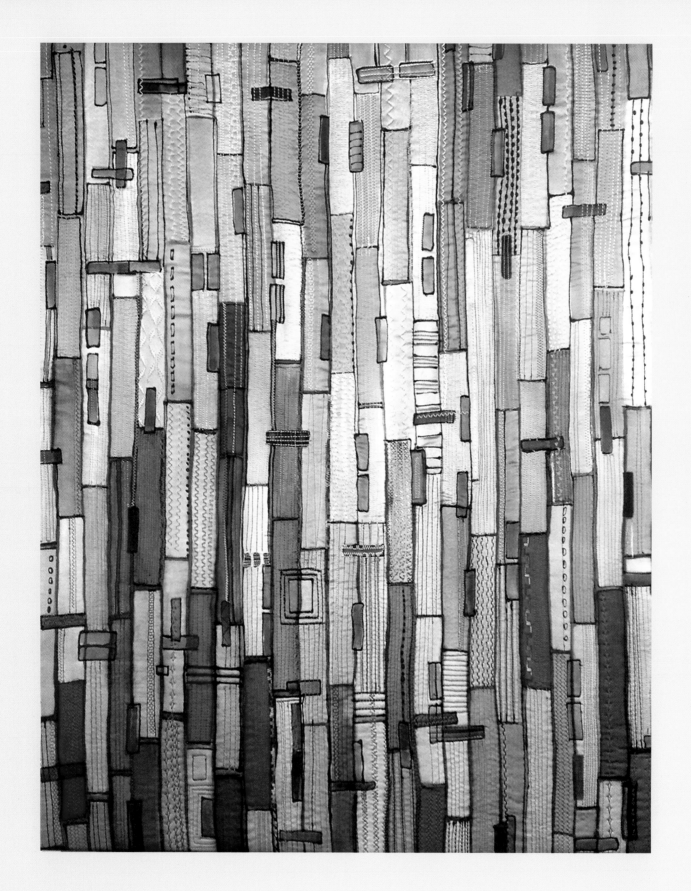

Mary Volin

Maine, USA.
Urban Twilight. 2013. 30" × 24".
Silk charmeuse, paint, dye, resist.
Silk painted, machine quilted.

Denise Oyama Miller

California, USA.
Scission. 2012. 30" × 24".
Cotton, repurposed watercolor painting, paint.
Mixed media collage, machine quilted.

Beth Carney

New York, USA.
Chasms 8. 2012. 36" × 36".
Hand-dyed cotton. Machine pieced, fused,
machine quilted. | Photo: James Dee.

Barbara Oliver Hartman

Texas, USA.
A Complete Unknown. 2008. 45" × 45".
Hand-dyed cotton, acrylic and wool yarn.
Machine appliqué, machine quilted, couched.

Catharine Stonard

Surrey, UK.
Lavender Fields Triptych. 2015. 12" × 27".
Cotton, inks, crayons, yarn. Hand painted, free motion
quilted, couched, hand stitched.

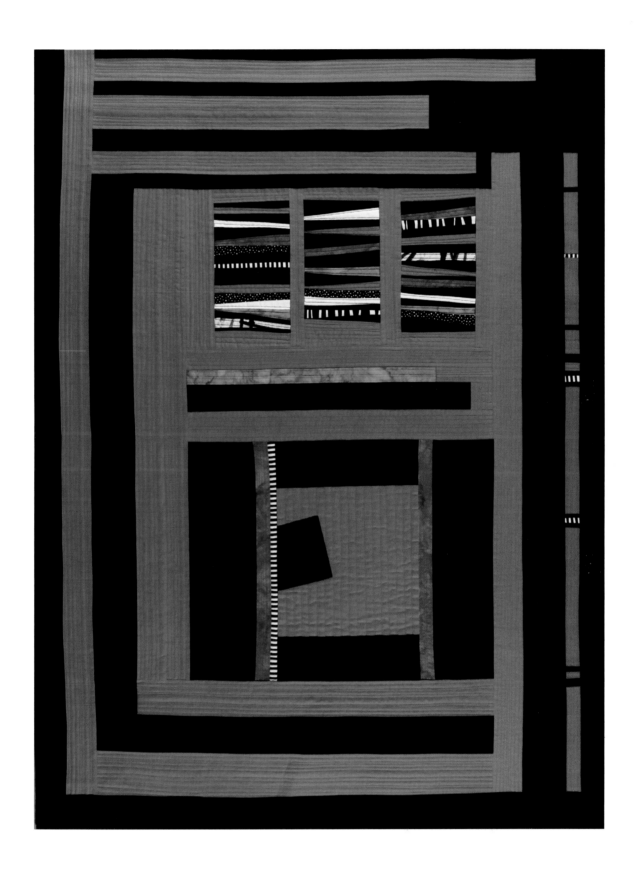

Hope Wilmarth

Texas, USA.
Intersections. 2012. 50" × 38".
Cotton. Machine pieced and quilted.
Photo: Rick Wells.

Marieke Steenhorst

Flevoland, the Netherlands.
Snow on my bedspread (based on a haiku by Kobayashi Issa: "Gratitude for gifts,
even snow on my bedspread, a gift from the Pure Land"). 2013. 51" × 38".
Organza, cotton, felt, plastic. Hand cut circles, machine stitched between layers
of organza, some of which has been melted away.
Photo: M.V. Steenhorst and J. J. Drop.

Simona Peled

Tel Aviv, Israel.
Choices. 2010. 65" × 34".
Cotton. Chenille, appliquéd, machine
and hand quilted. | Photo: Ran Erde.

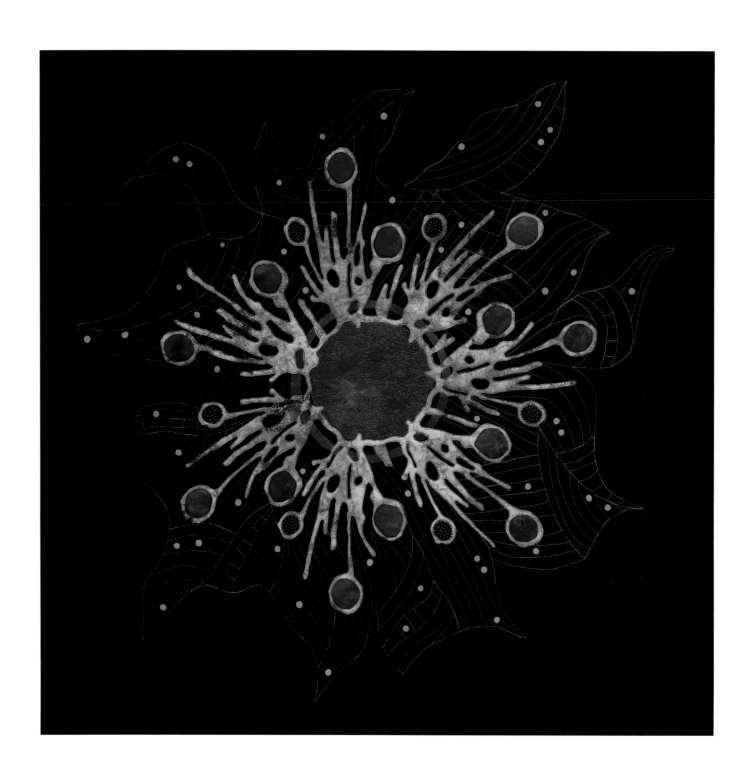

Charlotte Bird

California, USA.
Fruiting Body #9. 2012. 42" × 43".
Hand-dyed and commercial cotton. Hand-cut and -fused
appliqué, machine appliquéd, machine quilted, hand em-
broidered. | Photo: Eric Nancarrow.

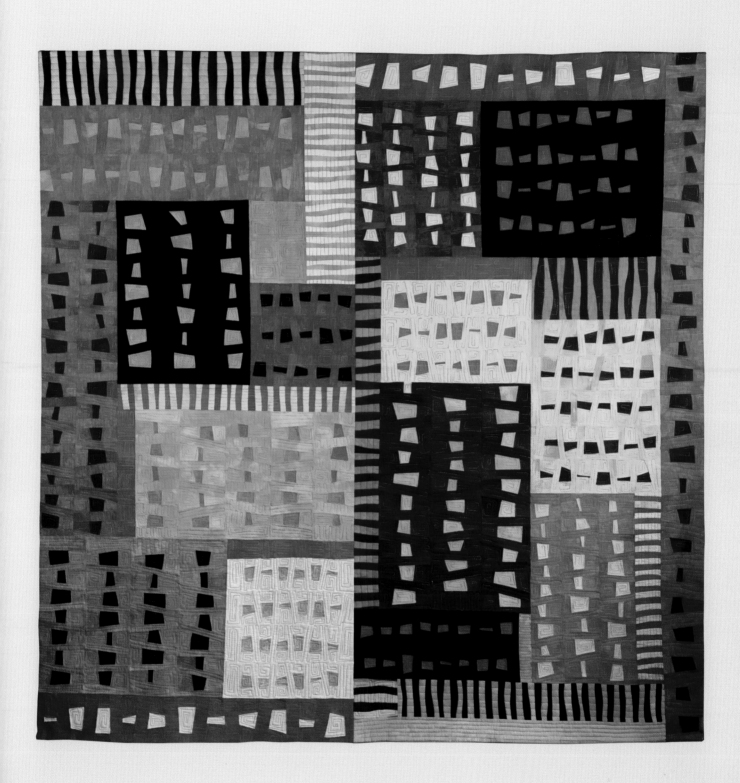

Norma Schlager
Connecticut, USA.
Salsa City. 2008. 52" × 50".
Hand-dyed cotton. Free form cut, pieced,
free motion quilted.

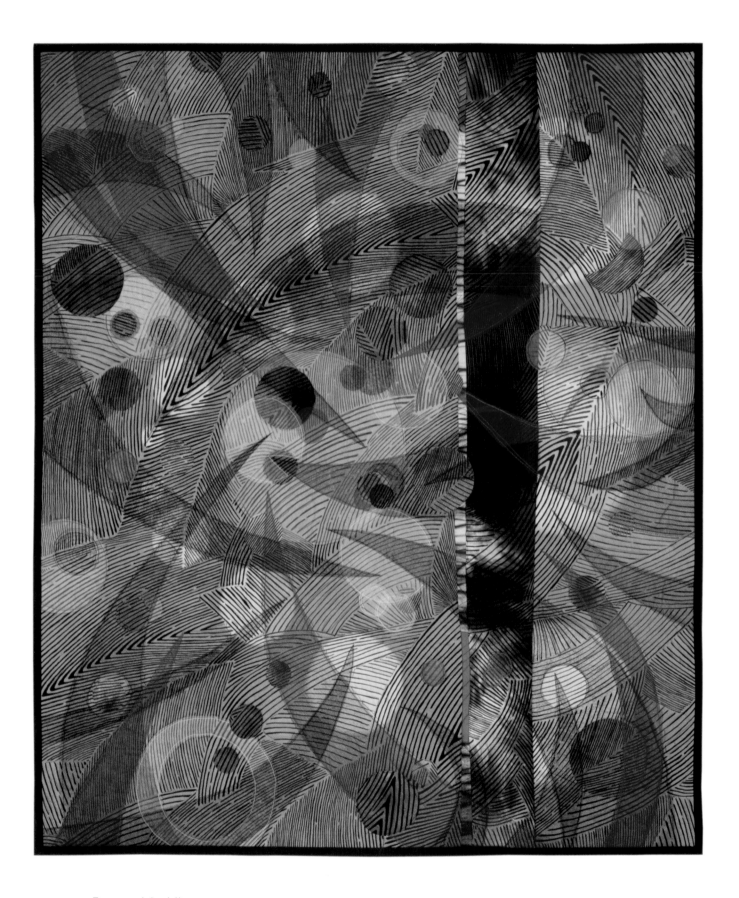

Jeanne Marklin
Massachusetts, USA.
Going in Circles. 2011. 38" × 32".
Hand-dyed cotton, organza, tulle. Shibori dyed, fused, pieced,
machine quilted. | Photo: Howie Levitz/TGL Photoworks.

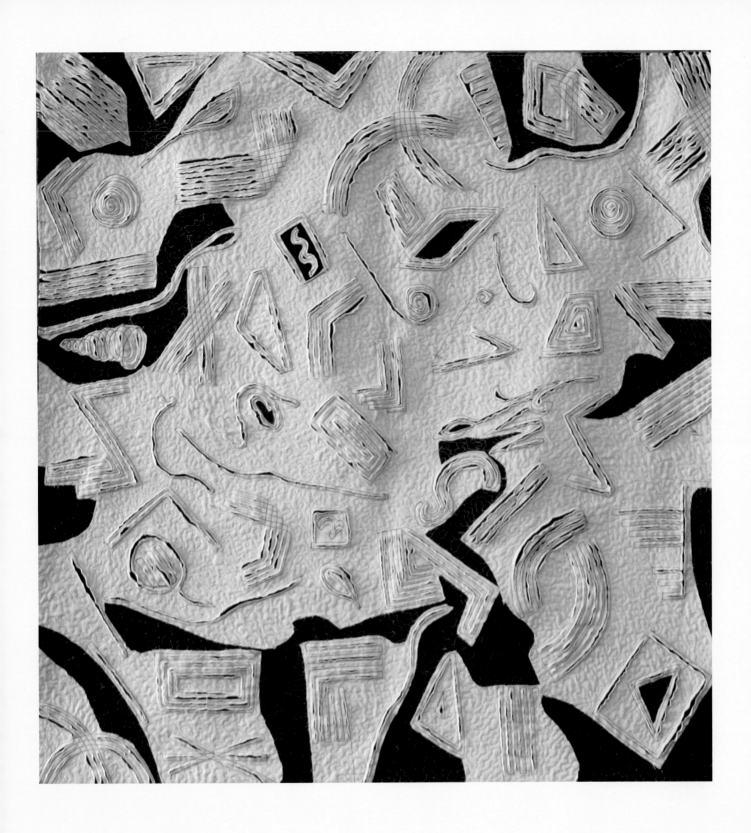

Francesca Sist

Pordenone, Italy.
Graffi (Scratches). 2012. 37" × 39".
Cotton flannel. Machine sewn,
machine and hand quilted.

Paul Schutte

Potchefstroom, South Africa.
Distortion: Polluted Ocean. 2014. 38" × 39".
Cotton, netting. Machine and hand pieced, machine
and hand quilted. | Photo: Alta Schutte.

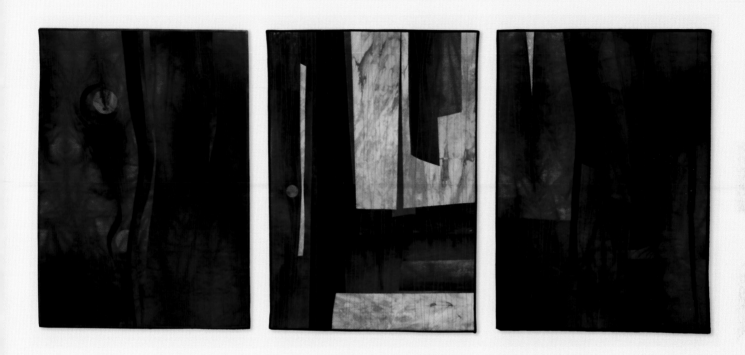

Joanne Alberda

Iowa, USA.
Triptych: Tales from a Ghost Town. 2011. 21" × 50".
Cotton. Collaged, machine stitched.

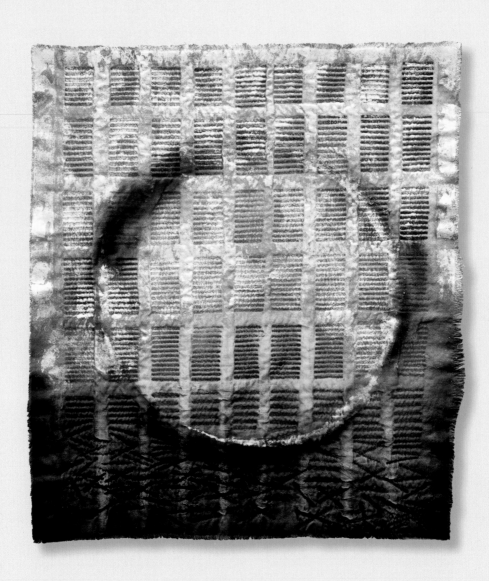

Kevan Lunney

New Jersey, USA.
Archeology Fragment #14, Enso. 2010. 54" × 48".
Linen, cotton, paint, metal leaf. Quilted, shrunk,
frayed, stenciled, painted, metal leaf application.
Photo: Marcia Schultz.

Leesa Zarinelli Gawlik

Colorado, USA.
Wandering Through. 2011. 32" × 47".
Silk, repurposed kimono. Dyed, reverse
appliquéd, machine embellished and stitched.
Photo: Petronella Ytsma.

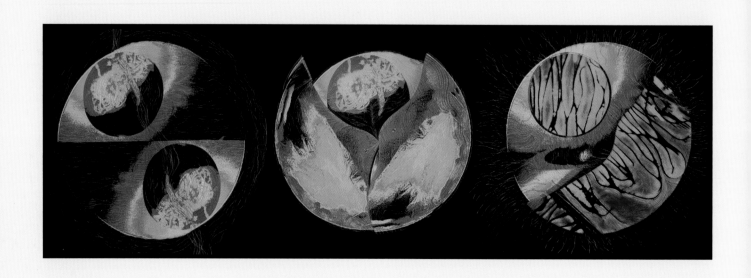

Barbara Schulman

Pennsylvania, USA.
Enigmatologist's Dream. 2012. 27" × 79".
Cotton, rayon. Manipulated digital images, discharged,
machine stitched. | Photo: John Sterling Ruth.

Ali George

Queensland, Australia.
Journey at 30,000 Feet. 2011. 22" × 21".
Cotton, buttons. Dyed with indigo and rust, machine and hand
pieced, hand embroidered and embellished, hand quilted.

Olga Prins Lukowski

Molenschot, the Netherlands.
Ups and Downs or Going with the Flow. 2014. 60" × 60".
Polyester organza, voile, colbach fiberglass fabric. Dyed, cut with soldering iron,
woven, machine stitched. | Photo: Peter Braatz, Studio Arnolds.

Kate Stiassni

Connecticut, USA.
A Tall Order. 2013. 37" × 48".
Hand-dyed cotton. Freehand cut, machine pieced
and stitched. | Photo: Avery Danziger.

Kate Findlay

Berkshire, UK.
Hidden Universe. 2012. 51" × 51".
Cotton, synthetics. Dyed, screen printed, pieced, couched,
machine embroidered. | Photo: Richard Sedgwick.

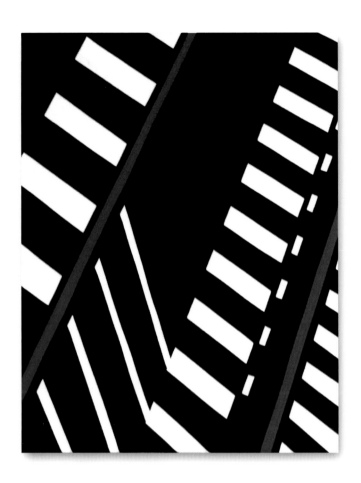

Linda Witte Henke

Indiana, USA.
Ebony and Ivory. 2010. 25" × 64".
Cotton. Machine pieced, machine stitched.
Photo: Phil Henke.

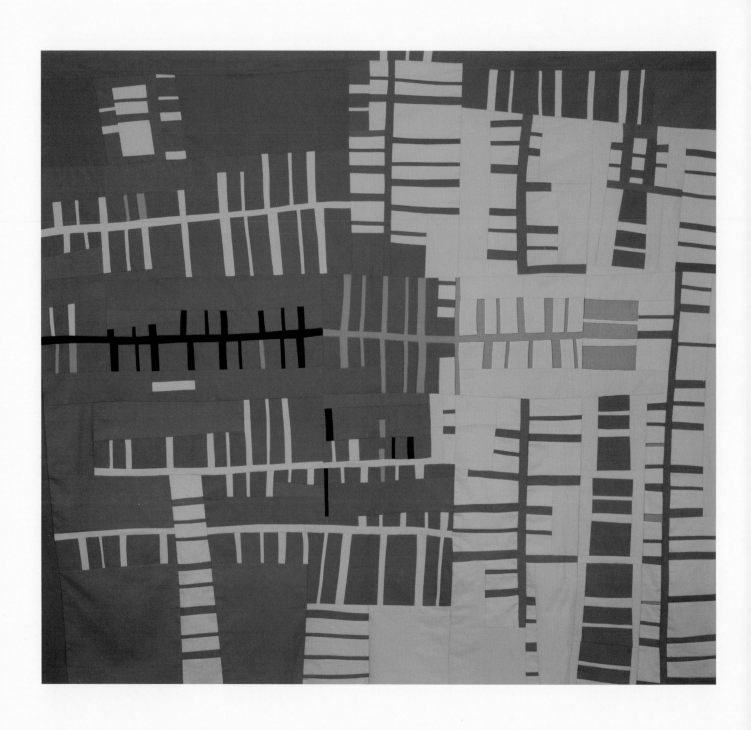

Gerri Spilka

Pennsylvania, USA.
City Edge #1. 2011. 58" × 54".
Cotton. Machine pieced and quilted.

Joan Sowada

Wyoming, USA.
Spice. 2013. 32" × 15". Canvas, cotton, paint. Painted, fused,
machine pieced and quilted. | Photo: Ken Sanville.

Janine Ayres
Kent, UK.
Light! Light! 2013. 35" × 30".
Cotton sateen, silk organza, dye, ink. Dyed, machine and hand quilted.

Jean Wells

Oregon, USA.
High Desert VIII. 2013. 43" × 24".
Hand-dyed and commercial cotton. Pieced and machine quilted.
Photo: Paige Vitek.

Denyse Schmidt

Bridgeport, Connecticut, USA

Widely credited with being a major inspiration for the modern quilt movement, Denyse Schmidt's realization that the contemporary decorating aesthetic needed a quilt style to match led to the founding of a successful business. Featuring traditional quilt motifs in a severely pared-down, minimalist format, Schmidt's art combines the quirky delight of found fabrics with a trained eye for composition and balance.

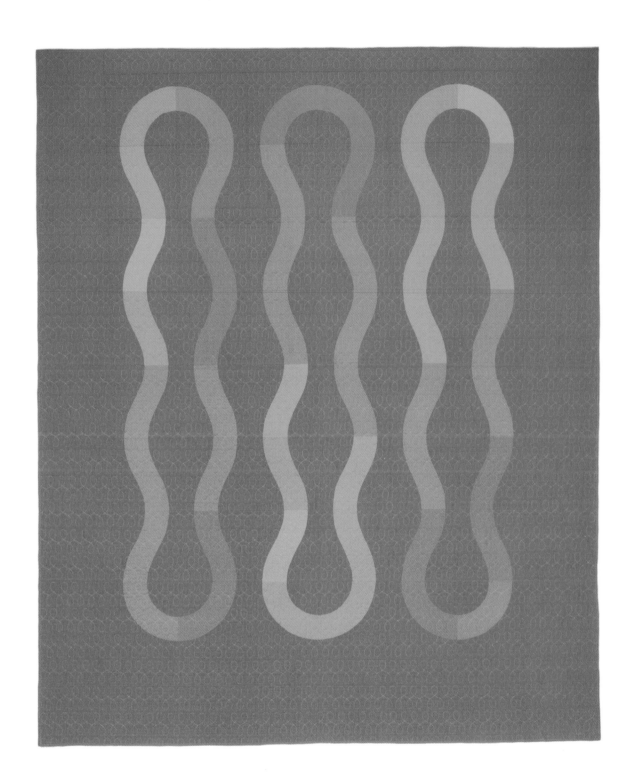

OPPOSITE *Hope as the Anchor of the Soul, Mt. Lebanon #3.* 2010. 93" × 86". Cotton, linen. Machine pieced, hand quilted by Julie Tebay. | Photo: Gamma One Conversions.

Snake Charmer. 2014. 88" × 66". Cotton. Hand appliquéd, hand quilted by Julie Tebay. | Photo: John Gruen.

The roads not taken

Between high school and starting Denyse Schmidt Quilts, I held a variety of jobs and studied graphic design at the Rhode Island School of Design. Among other employment, I worked as a cashier, theater prop assistant, costume shop assistant, receptionist, waitress, modern dancer, actress, performance artist, entrepreneur/jewelry designer, model, seamstress, retail associate, hostess, and graphic designer. Waitress, seamstress, and graphic designer repeated in various forms.

Design approaches

I think and dream with pencil and paper. My first ideas are captured in this way, as it's faster and easier to catch ideas as they form. If an idea feels worth exploring further, using the computer to draw the design to scale makes the transition to a life-size quilt much easier. With fabric designs, I draw on the computer from the get-go, since it's the only way I can then look at different colors. For me, coloring is the most important aspect of designing fabric.

Importance of quilting to design

Time and cost constraints determine whether a quilt is machine or hand quilted. As a designer, I'm happy to work within parameters and know before the process begins which method I will use. I love both very simple quilting patterns and ones that are complex. I love the qualities of hand quilting—the sense that it's being handmade, the texture it provides. I can experiment more with hand-quilting patterns since I draw the quilting lines directly on the quilt top. For most of my machine quilting, I rely on a figure eight pattern—it's neutral, an overall pattern with a soft even texture, and a

ready-made pattern I can rely on for good results from my quilter. I would love to get "behind the wheel" one day and explore hand-guided machine quilting that captures my drawing style, but it hasn't been feasible for me to add that to my schedule. Angela Walters did the quilting for *Centerline,* and it was gratifying to be able to describe a more complicated pattern and to see it executed so beautifully.

Love of antique quilts

I particularly love antique quilts that are spare or restrained. It is much more difficult to keep to a simple palette or pattern, and it's very easy to give in to the desire to add more, to use that as a crutch. So I have great respect for those makers who had or have the courage or discipline to stay the course, to let a single idea shine instead of throwing it all in at once. I also have a great fondness for quirky quilts that authentically reflect the hand or personality of the maker. By this I mean quilts that aren't trying to be perfect, but rather the quilts that are beautiful because of their quirks or "imperfections."

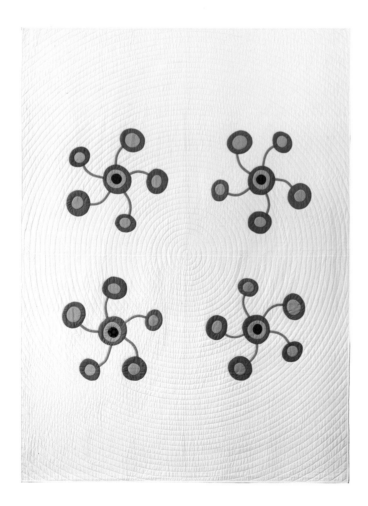

ABOVE *4 Crosses*. 2013. 93" × 86".
Cotton. Machine pieced, machine quilted by Janice Roy.
Photo: John Gruen.

LEFT *Swirly Rose*. 2005. 88" × 66".
Cotton. Hand appliquéd, hand quilted by Julie Tebay.
Photo: John Gruen.

Color

I believe we all have our own inner color tiller, and we have to first learn to recognize and then trust these inclinations. It's when we second-guess or try to follow what we think is "right" or trendy that things get all muddled. I have always had a strong sense of what I like color-wise. I think it's this confidence that people respond to most. In general I tend toward a warm palette—orangey reds and yellowy greens—but I am not tied to only producing work that reflects this. I don't adhere to any color theory other than to trust your own instincts.

How to judge quality

Looking and seeing is the only way to know. If I am not happy with how a quilt or fabric design looks, the only way past this is to uncover what is not working by trying other solutions.

Anything that changes your perspective can be a tool that helps you see more clearly. It can sometimes be a challenge, and no one is immune to it, but it is part of the creative process. I wish I could say it gets easier, but somehow it is always the same. It is less painful if you give yourself over to it and accept that design is a process of trial and error, of getting out of your own way, and of knowing your tools.

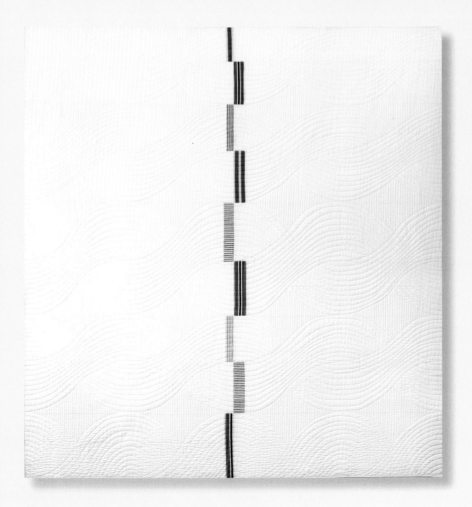

ABOVE *Stonehouse #1*. 2008. 86" × 93".
Cotton, waxed linen. Machine pieced, machine quilted by Janice Roy.

LEFT *Centerline*. 2013. 93" × 86".
Cotton. Machine pieced, machine quilted by Angela Walters. | Photo: John Gruen.

Jim Hay

Gunma, Japan

Jim Hay claims that his design style is a result of being born in Detroit, Michigan, the "Motor City." His works are certainly fast-paced, jam-packed with exciting imagery and explosive events. Life seems to be flying past at a great speed, filled with a multitude of intriguing symbols and enigmatic signs. The viewer is left breathless, trying to take it all in and make sense of the riotous imagery and pulsating action.

Your House Is on Fire. 2007. 91" × 87". Japanese kimono, various fabrics, cloth braid, rope. Appliquéd, machine stitched.

Dust to Dust. 2009. 90" × 90". Japanese kimono, various fabrics, lace. Appliquéd, machine stitched.

How I found Japan and quilting

I loved my American life. I started drawing at an early age and earned both BFA and MFA degrees. I was hired as a sculpture professor at Olivet College in Michigan and made many large artworks, including a five-ton cast bronze and stone "Tree of America" Bicentennial commission for Michigan.

In 1990 I jumped at the chance to be part of a two-week Sister Cities Conference in Japan. They said, "Stay and teach." That was a quarter century ago. When my wife and I bought a new house, it had no curtains. So I decided to make some—my first time sewing. I discovered that cloth was fun and full of potential. Cloth could be folded up and shipped easily to exhibitions around the world. Being able to put cloth artworks in a drawer between exhibitions is akin to rolling up Japanese scrolls. It made sense.

Design process

I usually work on only one piece at a time. My thoughts need to stay completely focused so that answers can come even during rest and sleep. I seldom do preliminary drawings or have specific expectations. I want to keep the doors open for continual creative discovery. If I need a bird, I pick up scissors and start cutting around a piece of cloth. No sketches, no drawing on the cloth. I trust. This will be my bird on this day.

Ideas come in flurries, so I must cut and sew quickly to allow the images to be revealed. As a child I knew every car as they raced past my house. I loved cars and motorcycles, loved driving fast and taking risks. For me, the foot pedal on a sewing machine has the same feel as the gas pedal on a car. I want to go fast, race around the cloth, and skid around corners—raise dust. Technique and craft are in perfect harmony with the intentions of the piece. Art is my personal path to awareness and communication of that awareness to others.

Natural Elements series

I made *Your House Is on Fire* with no intention of doing a series. Usually when I complete a piece, that part of my life is over. I move on, not knowing anything about what idea or even material may come next. *Your House Is on Fire* opened a wonderful new chapter, the challenge to do a series of *Natural Elements*. *Dust to Dust* is part of that series.

Fire is a major influence on the evolution of man but is less visible in our modern world: we turn up a thermostat for heat or turn on a burner to cook. The human spirit still responds to fire, just count the pyrotechnic displays in an action movie. Sadly, fire also fills our nightly TV news: suicide bombings, rockets wreaking havoc on cities, explosions ruining an evening with friends. This piece speaks to that destructiveness and that fear. *Your House Is on Fire* is neither friendly nor pretty. It doesn't boast of craftsmanship or lovely technique. It is rough. It is full of conflict. It doesn't whisper. It shouts. It screams. It burns.

ABOVE Jim Hay. *Wedding in the Wind*. 2008. 87" × 87". Japanese kimono, various fabrics, cloth images of Presidents Clinton and Bush. Appliquéd, machine stitched.

LEFT *August 10, 1912 Tomato Soup*. 2014. 46" × 46". Kimono and obi cloth, Gunma meisen silk, neckties, pencil, ink, canvas, photos and words printed on cloth, lace, transparent cloth, American glossy cloth, colored thread, ribbon. Drawn, printed, machine stitched.

Family stories

We are a regular family that has encountered a lot of irregular situations. For instance, my mother was only three when my grandparents purchased tickets for the *Titanic* but had to trade them in just before their departure when my great-grandmother became hospitalized. So they were not on the boat when it hit the iceberg and sank. They came the following year, settling in Detroit. I have used these stories and others as the inspiration for a new series, which includes *August 10, 1912 Tomato Soup* and *1953 Popcorn*.

Creation

If a piece isn't going well, I will cut it up. Some works are pinned but never sewn. One piece waited thirteen years. Tension filled our world after 9/11. I had started a piece called *Tightrope* in 2001, but set it aside as too painful. I finally completed it in 2014, and it won Third Place Original at the 2015 Tokyo International Great Quilt Festival.

Creation is a process both quick and slow. Quick: cut, don't draw, sew fast. Split-second decisions bring creative possibilities. Slow: keep creative during long months of construction. Move images, add, delete. Trust solves problems. Go to sleep. There will be a new answer by morning. Observe miracles.

ABOVE *1953 Popcorn*. 2014. 46" × 32".
Gunma meisen silk, canvas, photos printed on cloth, Japanese kimono and obi, various fabrics, lace, ribbon. Appliquéd, photo transfer, machine stitched.

LEFT *Tightrope*. 2014. 92" × 89".
Japanese kimono and obi cloth, Gunma meisen silk, my old shirt, bandolier toy gun belt and bullets, lace, ink, found objects. Appliquéd, braided rope, machine stitched.

Susie Koren

East Sussex, UK

There's a dynamic rhythm to Susie Koren's black and white compositions. The repetitive lines form patterns similar to a musical percussion section, while the swirls and loops of handwritten text create a poetic melody that builds around the underlying beats. Hand-stitched marks add grace notes that complete the visual symphony.

Inspiration

My work starts with the seed of an idea, often as I walk in the woods or on the coast. I am inspired by lines; the emptiness of bleak winter landscapes, silhouetted bare branches, frost icicles, stormy windswept beaches, marks in the sand, sea walls, grasses blowing in the wind, the colors of the earth, and meditation readings.

I have two hardback sketchbooks at all times and often reference previous sketchbooks. My A4 studio sketchbooks are not neat books, but working books with scribbles of ideas that come to mind for work in progress and future projects. There are sketches, annotated working drawings, templates and techniques, stuck in fabric and stitch samples, images, ideas for mark making, references to other artists, exhibitions, and books.

I always carry one of my smaller pocket sketchbooks to note down anything that inspires me. There are notes from exhibitions, watercolor sketches and line drawings from walks, rubbings of pigment, artists and designers that interest me, websites, color references, thoughts, feelings, moods. There is no sequence to these books and lots of bits stuck into them.

OPPOSITE *Keeping Still*. 2011. 35" × 46".
Cotton, silk organza. Batik, discharged, collaged, hand stitched. | Photo: Leslie Morgan.

Memories. 2010. 16" × 38".
Cotton, silk organza, feathers. Batik, discharged, collaged, hand stitched.

Mark making

Batik is a traditional Javanese (Indonesian) technique of using wax as a resist on cloth before dyeing it. The wax prevents the dye from coloring the cloth. Traditionally, the cloth is either printed with wax using copper stamps (tjaps) or drawn on directly using a special metal tool (tjanting) that has a reservoir bowl for holding the hot wax and a small spout/nib that is used to draw lines or dots on the cloth.

I work on black cotton cloth using a batik technique, but rather than using a tjanting I use a homemade nibbed pen and stamp the wax using found objects. To create very fine lines, I use a tiny Ukrainian wax tool originally designed for decorating Easter eggs. When the waxwork is finished, I discharge it with bleach and then rinse it in hot water to remove the black dye and wax before neutralizing the cloth against the bleach. I use soy wax that does not contain paraffin.

I employ a variety of methods to make marks in the wax: drawing, scratching, stamping, and writing with homemade tools or found objects. Then I discharge the color with various items, such as sponges and scouring brushes. These techniques create the subtle tones and marks on the background cloth that inspire my hand stitching. Some of the marks are made fast and freely, while others are slow and repetitive.

Obstruction. 2012. 40" × 52".
Cotton, silk noil. Batik, discharged, collaged, hand stitched. | Leslie Morgan.

Gravitational Force 1687. 2014. 43" × 59".
Cotton. Monoprinted with raw earth pigment and soy milk, stitched. | Photo: Leslie Morgan.

Color and thread

My favorite palette is a combination of neutral tones with a splash of color, red in particular, that gives my work a subtle Eastern quality. I have tried other colors but the red and ochre palette works best. A trip to Roussillon, France, introduced me to a variety of natural earth pigments. My new work, including *Gravitational Force*, is made using these pigments, which give me a broader but still muted palette that I am enjoying.

I Ching

The *I Ching*, also known as the Book of Changes, is an ancient Chinese Confucian book of divination that is made up of sixty-four "hexagrams" (basically sixty-four different arrangements of six rows of lines) that are interpreted in terms of yin and yang. British artist Richard Long used one of the hexagrams on the wall in an exhibition at Tate Britain, and I loved the simplicity and balance that the lines gave his composition. I do not pretend to begin to know how to interpret the book, but I found from studying it that I was drawn visually to the arrangement of the lines for certain hexagrams.

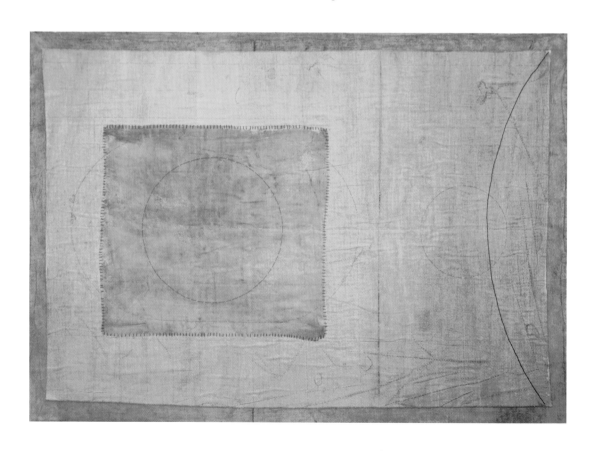

I was drawn to "obstruction" initially by the visual lines of that hexagram. The words and their placement create meaning, and the repetitive use of them became a mantra that helped me work through an artistic block and find balance. Traditionally a bundle of fifty yarrow sticks/stalks (from the yarrow plant) were used to consult the *I Ching*. I wanted to incorporate the yarrow sticks visually into the work, so I used the long stitches in bundles to form the hexagram for "obstruction"; the words are also written into the piece.

When I include words in a piece, the text is not intended to be legible. However the words and their meaning are in the work. If I want printed text in a piece, I use torn paper laminated onto a sheer medium, which gives a subtle result. *Union* was made the year of my twenty-fifth wedding anniversary and does not exactly fit into the *I Ching* series. I consciously chose the word "union" rather than being drawn visually by the hexagram. The circle represents eternity.

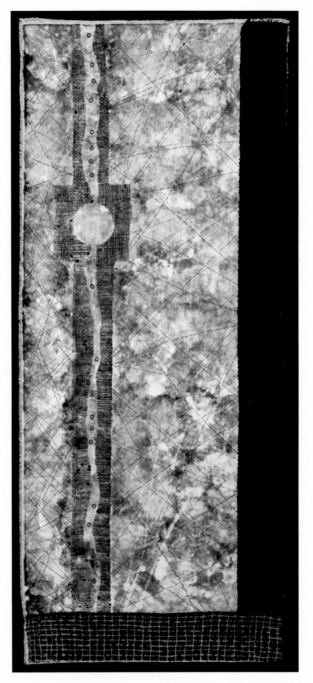

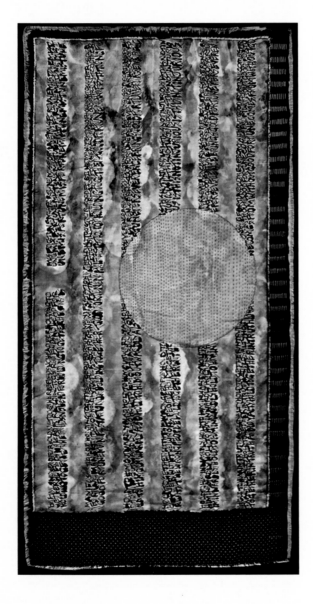

ABOVE *Pathways*. 2011. 40" × 21".
Cotton, silk noil, metal washers. Batik, discharged, collaged, hand stitched.

LEFT *I Ching Union*. 2012. 41" × 20".
Cotton, silk noil. Batik, discharged, collaged, hand stitched. | Photo: Leslie Morgan.

Judy Martin

Manitoulin Island, Ontario, Canada

Known for her dense hand stitching, Judy Martin's art explores the process of making. Working in cloth is a form of meditation, as thousands of stitches slowly cover the surface and piece together a new beginning.

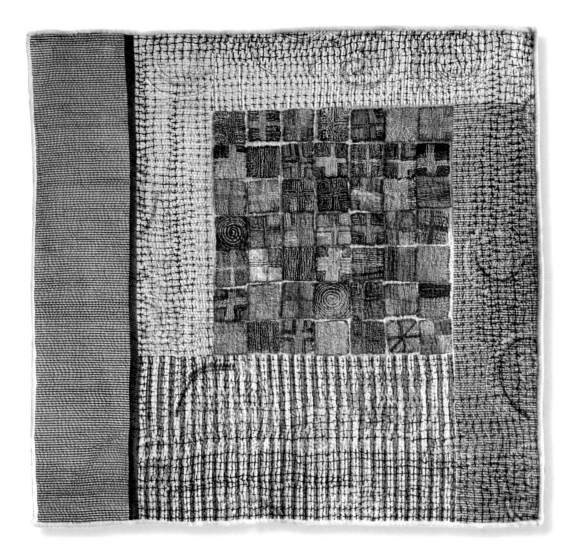

Process not product

Making something slowly with one's hands is perhaps one of the most nourishing things a person can do. Creating something from nothing—or better, creating something new from something no longer needed or wanted—is healing for the planet and for us.

The Manitoulin Circle Project was a sewing circle that met every week to create four ninety-inch-square panels. One of the four panels, *Mended World*, uses a variety of donated and thrift shop damask table linens string-pieced together, cut, and pieced again. Because of the multiple seams, the narrow strings often had to be mended using backstitching as they were being pieced together. As I worked to mend an area of the central circle, the title *Mended World* came to me as a description of the form we were stitching, as well as a vision of hope for our planet. I think that these panels give hope. These panels are solid; they are real. They are a tangible way to show our belief in a future.

Importance of solitude

Growing up in an isolated rural environment has greatly affected my life, my worldview, and certainly my work. I grew up on 160 acres in northern Ontario, miles from any kind of civilization. Isolation is familiar for me and maybe it's even necessary. I grew up with my two siblings and a lot of solitude. Summers were spent under the willow trees daydreaming.

Today I choose to live in the country and try to spend most days alone. My work reflects this choice and often references what I live with here on Manitoulin Island: large empty fields of grass, long views over ripples of water toward a calm horizon.

OPPOSITE *Mended World*. 2013. 94" × 94".
Repurposed linen and cotton damask, silk, cotton. Hand pieced, machine pieced, hand quilted, hand embroidered. Made with community assistance as part of the Manitoulin Circle Project. Photo: Klaus Rossler.

Cross My Heart. 2010. 33" × 35".
Silk, linen, velvet, dye, paint. Layered, pieced, embroidered, hand quilted.

Hand stitching is a time for reflection

My art is about relationships: with family, with nature, and with my inner self. My art is the only place where I feel I can express these things and communicate about them on a deep level. Repetition of simple small stitch marks over a large area can be powerful. In 2010, I was startled by how old I was going to be and felt the necessity to mark each day of my sixtieth year. Every day I used up an entire skein of embroidery floss and some of the fabrics that I'd been keeping safe.

I kept going, stitching every day for three complete years, ending the work on my sixty-second birthday. Part of me wanted to keep doing it for the rest of my life; the other part of me needed to stop spending so much of my valuable time on *Not to know but to go on*. Three years gave me 220 feet. That was enough.

Art is an adventure

In the spring and summer of 2014, I harvested and processed local plants here on Manitoulin in order to dye yards of reclaimed blanket-weight wool fabric. Stitching the wool, transforming it from something meaningful in its own right to something that used all of those qualities but added the emotion and self-revelation that art brings, was more challenging than I expected. How does one keep the work simple and pared down when working with such luxurious materials?

Beginning with Time is filled with dense, ordered columns of seed stitch in wool yarns. I hope that what my work communicates is the quiet joy of making and at the same time the feeling that we are each just a tiny speck. As it progressed, the piece took on a stubborn silent quality. It would not be defeated. The dots below the horizon are perhaps the safety net I think about or represent a depth we cannot fathom. There is no eye level focal point. Instead, it evokes a feeling of being lost in the woods. The comfort usually associated with wool blankets is altered and gravity is created: the heavy materials and dark colors have an emotional gravity as well as a physical one.

OPPOSITE

ABOVE *Not to know but to go on*. 2013. 223 feet × 14".
Canvas, found fabrics, cotton floss, cotton tape; hand stitched. | Photo: Gareth Bate.

LEFT *Beginning with Time: Day*. 2015. 78" × 90".
Repurposed wool blanket, dye, cotton floss. Dyed, hand stitched. | Photo: Nick Dubecki.

RIGHT *Beginning with Time: Night* Reverse of *Day*.
78" × 90".
Repurposed wool blanket, dye, cotton floss. Dyed, hand stitched. | Photo: Nick Dubecki.

Fragile as a Leaf. 2004. 98" × 73".
Cotton, linen, dye, embroidery floss, sequins. Shibori dyed, pieced, appliquéd, reverse appliquéd, hand embroidered.
Photo: Sarah Warburton.

Power of cloth

I believe that my work in textiles reaches others on a more emotional level than drawing or painting ever can. The reason for this is the very materiality of cloth and stitch. Cloth has a most intimate connection to the human body. Babes are wrapped in cloth within minutes of emerging from the womb. Cloth is fragile and wears out with age, like the human body. The hand stitch is a slow method of making a mark and seems to hold time and make it visible. This time spent repeatedly touching a piece expresses a thoughtful caring and tenderness. There is power in cloth that has been stitched by hand.

Aina Muze

Riga, Latvia

84

Geometric simplicity gives power to Aina Muze's art. Trained as a tapestry artist, she brought a similar aesthetic to her work in art quilts and has been instrumental in training several generations of Latvian artists in the medium. Her work is built from a combination of a subdued palette, celebration of the fabric's inherent beauty, and compositions created from the strength of repeating forms.

Background in tapestry

I completed my studies at the Textile Department of the Latvian Academy of Arts. From 1967 until 1993, I participated in many tapestry exhibitions. I created commissioned works for significant state institutions, as well as for private interiors. My tapestries are in the collections of museums in Latvia and Russia, and in numerous private collections. My tapestries can also be found in church interiors in Latvia, Denmark, and Sweden.

After the establishment of the independent state of Latvia in the beginning of the 1990s, the art scene changed and the number of exhibitions decreased. During that time I had an opportunity to travel abroad, and I saw what was being done in patchwork and quilting. The techniques aroused my interest, and I decided to give them a try.

The Textile Department at the Latvian Academy of Arts was very interested in the body of work that I developed and decided to include patchwork and quilting in their study program. I was invited to be the teacher. And now, after more than twenty years, several generations of young artists have developed their own individual art quilt styles. Art quilts have become more and more popular among these artists and in Latvia generally.

In 2011, I was one of the founders of the Latvian Quilt Association. We hold an annual festival as an opportunity for members to show their accomplishments. It has become an international quilt festival (www.latviaquilting.lv), and in 2012 the Latvian Quilt Association became a member of the European Quilt Association.

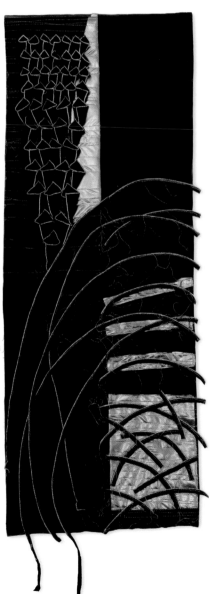

OPPOSITE *Bolero*. 2003. 51" × 51". Wool, cotton, linen, synthetics, silk, lace, tulle. Appliquéd, machine quilted, stitched, embroidered.

LEFT *Language of Frost*. 2007. 68" × 23". Wool, metallic fabric. Appliquéd, machine stitched. | Photo: Armands Lacis.

RIGHT *Façade*. 2008. 68" × 27". Linen, cotton, synthetic fabric. Machine stitched and embroidered.

Pleasure of old linen

I enjoy working with old linen fabrics due to their distinct textures. I always use linen if it will help to reveal the idea behind the work. I especially use old linen in my works about history, such as *Linen Series* and *Interchange of Centuries*. By no means am I using the term "old" in the sense of worn or used. I inherited several bolts of one-hundred-year-old, handwoven linen. The fabrics are unique and cannot be bought anywhere today.

Importance of music

I always listen to music while I am working. My work *Bolero* is an homage to Ravel. Ravel's music is closely connected with the dance genres, especially the bolero and the waltz. Part of my work is an improvisation on the process of writing music, so it is filled with blank music papers, musical lines, and handwriting. The other part of the work shows the transformation of the music into dance. Many layered circles represent the whirling dancers.

Fascination with architectural forms

Architecture is another of my favorite themes. I love to travel, and while travelling I pay very special attention to the architecture. This is an inexhaustible source of inspiration: the textures of the walls of houses or other historical buildings, imprints on the pavements, interiors of monasteries with faded wall paintings and mosaics. I take many photos and use them as a source for ideas for new quilts. *Façade* is from a series about architecture. I am fascinated by ancient architecture especially in contrast to modern buildings of glass and metal. I try to reflect these impressions in my work using different materials and techniques.

Design basics

The basic geometric forms—circle, square, triangle—are of utmost importance in the progression of my work, as well as in developing designs. I love to study architecture and human history. In both areas, one can see how these shapes are organized into specific visual rhythms.

ABOVE *Linen Series*. 2009. 50" × 43".
Linen, cotton, lace. Appliquéd, machine stitched and quilted. Photo: Armands Lacis.

LEFT *Inspiration*. 2006. 45" × 37".
Wool, cotton, linen, silk, lace, tulle. Appliquéd, machine stitched and quilted. | Photo: Armands Lacis.

OPPOSITE *Interchange of Centuries*. 2010. 58" × 46".
Felt, linen, cotton. Inkjet printed, appliquéd, machine and hand stitched. | Photo: Armands Lacis.

The beginning of a work for me might be very spontaneous without any special forethought. As a work progresses, I will add geometrical forms depending on the idea or theme of the particular work. While building a composition, I intuitively follow my understanding of these geometric forms, as well as the possibilities for their interpretation. Experiments for enriching the texture of the fabrics are possible through the application of various surface design techniques, such as silk-screen printing, inkjet printing, appliqué, and embroidery. Every one of these methods is very inspiring and helpful in revealing my ideas for a piece.

The development of a design is not always easy to foresee. I usually begin with the larger forms, gradually completing them with details and methods corresponding to the chosen theme. Sometimes everything falls into place, but there are times when changes occur repeatedly. Certainly, there are basic rules of composition, but there is no one specific definition. Design is everyone's unique and individual expression.

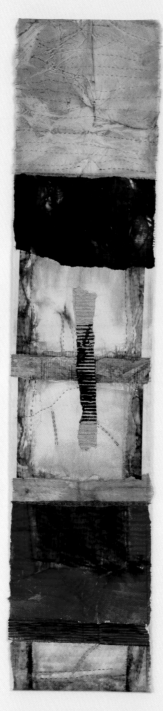

Elly van Steenbeek
Veenendaal, the Netherlands

While a grid of squares might suggest conformity or regimentation, Elly van Steenbeek's art is anything but. Pushing the square in new directions, her works are an autobiographical chronicle of her life, health, and emotions. Constant experimentation with the use of paper, dyeing using rust, and recently the addition of hand stitching, keep the work fresh and exciting.

Inspiration

Because of our two dogs, I spend a lot of time outside. We have a park nearby, which is my biggest source of inspiration. I translate the colors of the seasons into abstract designs in my art. An example is my work *Wintersong*, inspired by the sun shining on the water during winter. It was cold, the sun was orange, and you could see how golden it looked sparkling on the water.

My latest work is more emotional and more about my life. Maybe it's due to becoming older that emotions are more important in my art. However, I like to give my artworks a touch of happiness and joy, even when the subject isn't very cheerful. So I use my favorite colors: yellow, orange, and red. For me they mean happiness, joy, and power. Always look on the bright side of life.

While my new series is autobiographical, it's translated in a general abstract way. Last year I had to wait for surgery for eight months. The last months were tough, so I came up with the idea of *Waiting*. Nobody likes waiting. It's boring, and every day looks the same. This quilt is about three weeks of waiting; the same blocks are repeated in every section.

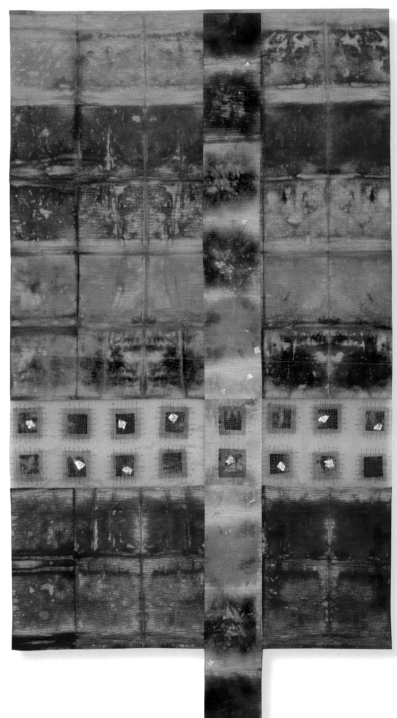

OPPOSITE *Waiting*. 2014. 47" × 35".
Cotton, painted found papers, found papers altered with rust and tea. Raw edge appliquéd, hand embroidered, hand quilted, machine stitched.
Photo: Geurt van Steenbeek.

Wintersong. 2013. 52" × 29".
Hand-dyed cotton, organza, painted paper. Machine stitched and quilted. | Photo: Geurt van Steenbeek.

Paper

I started making art quilts after taking a two-year course in Holland called "Quilten Speciaal." They introduced us to all sorts of materials, because they wanted everybody to get out of their comfort zone of using only patchwork blocks.

After that course I tried many materials, but from the start paper was my favorite. I got in contact with a paper mill, and I get papers from a clothing store (the wrapping papers from the clothes). I also collect all sorts of different papers that you can find around your house, such as from a box or carton, from foods, etc. I dye the papers with fiber reactive dyes and alter them with rust. It's a new challenge to discover all the possibilities available from different types of paper.

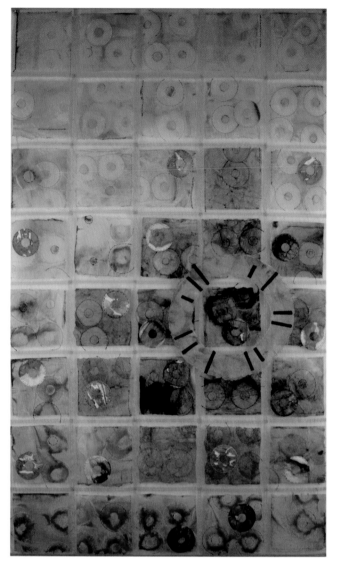

Squares

I use a grid of squares as the background for much of my work. As a practical matter, I create squares when I hand-dye my fabrics in the microwave. A few years ago I got some square plastic containers into which I place folded fabrics. This new way of dyeing and experimenting resulted in a lot of fabrics. For my fabrics dyed with rust, I use a square rusty tray. I've also done a lot of experiments with folded fabrics and discovered my own recipes.

For me, the square is a symbol for balance, structure, stability, and strength. These keywords are important for my life.

ABOVE *Life Story*. 2015. 49" × 30".
Rusted tissue paper, rubber, organza. Fused, torn, rusted, hand stitched. | Photo: Geurt van Steenbeek.

LEFT *The Red Line*. 2015. 36" × 24".
Cotton, polyester organza, paper. Paper lamination, appliquéd, machine stitched, hand embroidered.
Photo: Geurt van Steenbeek.

Design

I always start a new work based on an idea. Then I look in my stash to see which colors will fit with this subject. I have a design board on which I hang the different pieces of fabric together. Sometimes I will draw a design, but I don't use a sketchbook. I write notes on little white papers. They are everywhere in my house. It's a little messy, but it works for me.

The quilt starts to grow on my design board. Sometimes I don't feel what I wish to convey, so I start again with a new plan using new fabrics. Sometimes the quilt design is finished in a few hours; sometimes it takes a week or more. My emotional response is very important for me: can I tell the story behind it?

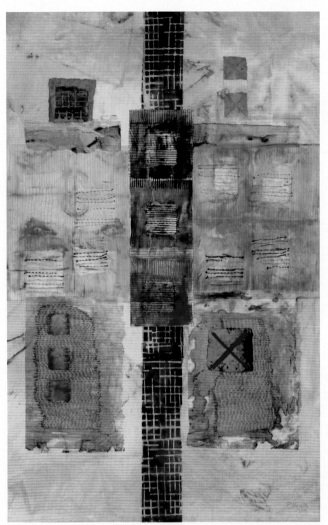

TOP RIGHT *We.* 2012. 46" × 29".
Cotton and tissue paper altered with rust and tea, painted papers. Monoprinted, hand stitched, machine stitched and quilted. Photo: Geurt van Steenbeek.

LEFT *Life Lines.* 2014. 49" × 39".
Hand-dyed cotton, painted paper. Machine stitched, raw edge appliquéd, machine quilted. | Photo: Geurt van Steenbeek.

Hand stitching

Most of the time a quilt will be hanging on my design board for about two weeks. I look at it every day and try to learn something more about it. I begin thinking about the quilting: straight lines or curves, by machine or by hand. My latest works are stitched by hand. This started by accident, because I couldn't work for a long time at my sewing machine. Nevertheless I wanted to make art, so I decided to do it by hand. It's much more fun than I expected. I like it so much that at this moment handwork is more important than working by machine. A new challenge.

I don't plan the hand stitches of my newest work. It just grows with every step I take. And I like this way of working. It is constantly exciting and surprising.

Judith Larzelere

Westerly, Rhode Island, USA

Judith Larzelere has been making art quilts for thirty-six years. Until the start of 2014, her signature strip-pieced designs focused on brilliant, saturated color combinations that reverberate visually. Currently immersed in an exploration of all-white quilts, Larzelere creates dazzling geometric designs in all color palettes.

Strip-piecing technique

My strip-piecing technique involves three main stages. In the first, I strip piece various widths of cloth into sheets, which are then recut perpendicular to the seams into one-inch bands. The second stage involves creating a "platform" of backing, batting, and muslin (or a batik-pieced design). All layers are hand basted together. In the third stage, I take the pieced bands and sew them one by one onto and through the platform layers so as to create a face side where no quilting stitching is visible. After assembly using this "flip and sew" method of quilting, I square up and trim the edges.

OPPOSITE *Red Volunteer*. 2006. 52" × 48".
Cotton. Strip pieced.

Melt. 2010. 60" × 96".
Cotton. Strip pieced.

Music and gardening

I guess the organized patterning and flow of notes on a staff are deeply imprinted on my brain because I started playing the piano when I was five years old. I'm not a very accomplished musician; I don't practice enough. However, I am sure the comfort I have with strip piecing and the look of it are connected to looking at musical scores and listening to complex polyphonic compositions.

When I'm not quilting, I'm usually in the garden. I feel so good when I am outdoors, so the gardening is a complement to the indoor work of quilting. I think I would have been unable to flourish as a human being or as an artist in the midst of a city. I must live most of my hours close to plants, animals, and the ocean.

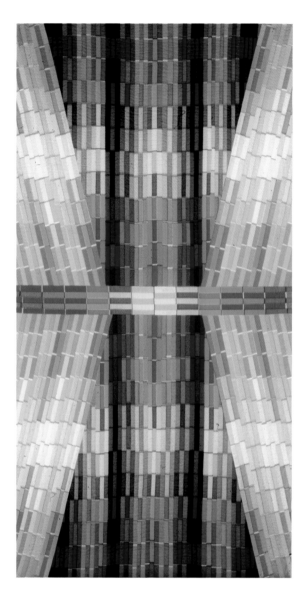

Color experiments

In the past, much of my choice of colors was made in pursuit of either eliciting a response in the mood of a viewer or trying to re-create color combinations seen in nature or in my garden. I also react to seasonal changes of color and of daylight and in the past would often choose a palette to incorporate or honor what I was seeing around me. I made hot-toned work in summer and paler work in mid-winter and spring. I used complementary colors for a visual kick and often made that the major theme of a composition.

Rippling Color is flat, not a three-dimensional structure. The startling dimensional effect is due to the application of color theory—in a given hue family, more saturated colors and darker value colors will visually advance over less saturated and lighter value colors.

Starting in 2010, I began experimenting with very minimalist quilts with limited palettes. I also eliminated the use of narrow accent bands. I found I could produce a vibrating color field with just a few fabrics instead of the thirty to fifty colors that I'd been using. I could even use a monochrome palette and still elicit an emotional response from viewers.

ABOVE *Rippling Color*. 1996. 86" × 44".
Cotton. Strip pieced.

RIGHT *Static Interference*. 2010. 64" × 60".
Cotton. Strip pieced.

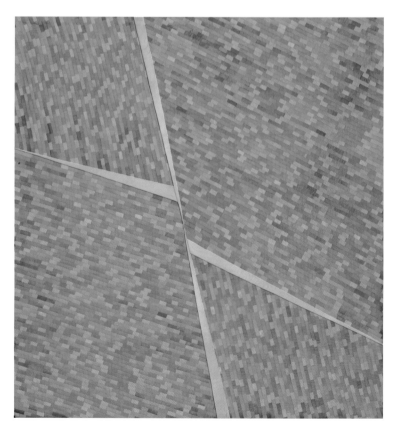

Experimenting with white

Currently, I am curious to see what happens in the near absence of color, what can be done near the boundary of perceptible color when combining reflective and matte surfaces to form patterns, and when translucency adds a mysterious overtone to a white on white work. The resulting quilts are not as flashy, but there is an ethereal beauty to my newest work.

Translucency and Kaleidoscope has four layers, not the traditional three, with white, translucent bands quilted on top of the other layers as they are sewn on. I used bleached white cotton twill for the backing, polyester batting, and a geometric pieced layer. The white on white bands combine reflective silk charmeuse and bamboo, with thin cottons and silks for translucency. Interestingly, with this piece, I'm now working back into complexity after a long time spent exploring very minimal approaches to quilt design.

It's like playing beautiful music

Strip quilting as I practice it is hard to correct in mid-course. Ripping out row after row of strip quilting is not an option I practice or recommend. Sometimes, colors just don't perform as I'd imagined and a jumble is made instead of something that falls into place. This can happen if I push into art making when I'm coming down with a cold, or if I'm worrying a lot about some extraneous problem outside of my studio life.

When a work goes well, it feels like playing a beautiful piece of music with expression and verve. It feels like writing a poem as the words form effortlessly out of the unconscious depths of the mind. It feels like swimming in a beautiful pool where the water is pure and just the right temperature.

ABOVE *Translucency and Kaleidoscope.*
2014. 58" × 60". Cotton. Strip pieced.

RIGHT *Luminosity: Teal, Coral, Gold.*
2011. 63" × 63". Cotton. Strip pieced.

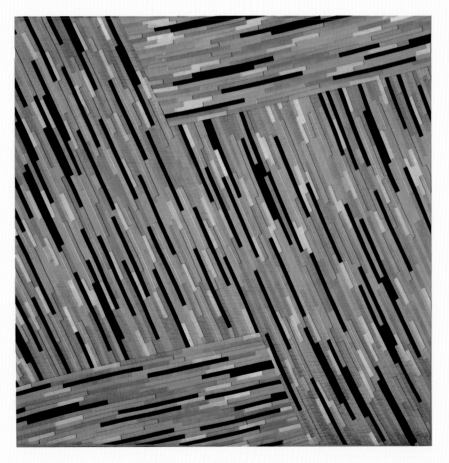

Sara Impey

Colchester, UK

Written words are probably the ultimate abstraction: we use a system of symbols (letters) to represent sounds and form words, which represent complex concepts and ideas. Sara Impey's body of work explores how words interact with the concepts they describe. Recent pieces take an increasingly sculptural approach to conveying exactly how and what we are trying to say.

A CHOREOGRAPHIC INSTALLATION FUSING MOVEMENT WITH DIGITAL PROJECTION TO CREATE A PERFORMANCE WITH SOUND AND INTERACTIVE MEDIA SEEMS AT FIRST TO HAVE LITTLE IN COMMON WITH THE SLOW AND TIME-HONOURED PROCESS OF MAKING QUILTS. ONE ARTFORM IS TECHNICALLY ADVANCED AND EXPERIMENTAL IN NATURE AND INVITES ITS VIEWERS TO CONFOUND THEIR NORMAL SENSORY EXPERIENCES BY CONJURING UP A FLUID WORLD IN WHICH LIVE DANCE MIXES WITH COMPUTER-HELD IMAGERY ALONG WITH MUSIC AND VOICES TO PRODUCE AN ATMOSPHERE THAT STIRS AND ENGAGES. IT DEPENDS ON ARTISTS FROM VARIOUS DISCIPLINES REHEARSING INTENSIVELY TO GENERATE A WORK THAT IS UNIQUE AND UNPREDICTABLE. BUT A QUILTER USUALLY STITCHES ALONE OVER A LENGTHY PERIOD SO HER QUILTMAKING GRADUALLY BECOMES INTERWOVEN IN HER MIND WITH MEMORIES CONNECTED TO THE EVENTS GOING ON IN HER LIFE AT THAT TIME. QUILTING IS A RELATIVELY LOW TECH AND DOMESTIC SKILL THAT RELIES ON MANUAL TECHNIQUES PRACTISED OVER MANY YEARS. IT REQUIRES METICULOUS AND CONSISTENT ACCURACY AND THE END PRODUCT – THE QUILT – MAY WELL LAST AND BE VALUED BY FUTURE GENERATIONS. IN BOTH FIELDS OF EXPRESSION THE IDEA OF SELF IS TEMPORARILY LOST IN THE CREATIVE AND TRANSFORMATIVE ACT OF MAKING OR STAGING AND PERFORMING. AT BEST A NARRATIVE UNFOLDS THAT ENGENDERS A MEANINGFUL CONVERSATION ... THE ARTIST AND THE AUDIENCE

OPPOSITE *No Exit*. 2013. 35" × 35".
Cotton. Wholecloth, machine quilted, free motion machine stitched text. | Photo: Kevin Mead.

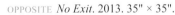

Process. 2009. 56" × 52".
Cotton. Hand dyed, wholecloth, machine quilted.
Photo: Peter Evans.

Chain Stitch. 2013. 15' × 2.5".
Silk. 25 mini-quilts linked in a chain, each one is wholecloth, free motion machine stitched. | Photo: Kevin Mead.

Hexagon beginnings

I never dreamt that sewing would feature so largely in my life. Needlework was my least favorite subject at school. However, my mother came from that wartime generation who made all their own clothes, and in 1971 when I was seventeen, she produced from nowhere a hexagon template. I had never come across such a thing before and was fascinated with the idea that sewing fabric over cardboard would stiffen it so that the patches could easily be stitched together. I spent a happy week sitting on the floor cutting up old shoeboxes for the cardboard templates and making a patchwork quilt from the fabric scraps she had amassed over the previous two decades. I still have this quilt, which contains samples from party dresses and nightdresses from my childhood, and from my mother's dresses, some of which date back to the 1950s and maybe even the 1940s.

My career was in journalism, and I was a reporter for the *Times* newspaper covering the Houses of Parliament. I love words and had wanted to use text in my work for some time. I began experimenting with text in 2004. I didn't want the text to be an add-on, but an integral part of the design. My first text-based quilts were simply lists of related words or reproduced verses from Victorian samplers. It was when I started stitching my own writing that I felt I had finally found my voice as a quilter—thirty years after making my first quilt.

Text vs. color and form

For me, the two elements—text and design—are inextricably linked. When thinking up ideas and planning the quilts, it's hard to know which comes first. I want the text to be legible and to mean something, and I want the overall design to relate to that meaning. Achieving this is quite hard and I don't always manage it. Over the years, the writing has become as important to me as the quilting.

For my quilts based on a grid, I need a simple font without serifs. I choose Arial Uppercase because all the letters are the same height with no ascenders or descenders and fit snugly within a square. Arial is a neutral font with no stylistic associations. I don't want people to be aware of the font—I just want the letters to look neat, consistent, and professional.

The text on the "handwriting" quilts, like *Between the Lines* and *Blue-Sky Thinking*, is not an existing font at all—it is my own free-machine-stitched handwriting, letter by letter. I use uppercase for the same reason as mentioned above—the letters are all the same height and fit between my quilted parallel lines.

Circles in squares

I started working with circles because they are visually so arresting and have a simple and universal appeal. The circles vary in prominence in different quilts as I experiment with different effects. I was thinking about Alzheimer's disease when I made *No Exit*. My mother-in-law died from it, and it's one of our deepest fears as we grow older. I first quilted the whole piece in a grid and then in concentric circles. I began stitching the text from the center and worked outwards, clearing a path to stitch by pushing the threads out of the way toward the middle. I was then able to comb the tangled mess of threads out from the center.

The thread ends are not secured in any way. The fibers cling to one another and to the background fabric and support their own weight. Every time this quilt is handled or rolled, I have to comb them out again, so it never looks quite the same. I was hoping to achieve a visual metaphor for the text. This was one occasion where the verbal, visual, semantic, and structural seemed to come together.

OPPOSITE Sara Impey. *Blue-Sky Thinking*. 2013. 50" × 50".
Cotton. Hand and machine pieced, machine quilted, free motion machine stitched text. | Photo: Kevin Mead.

LEFT *Following the Thread*. 2014.
Quilted tape: 28' × 0.75"; Spool: 14" × 8".
Calico, found spool. Machine pieced, free motion machine stitched text. | Photo: Peter Evans.

RIGHT *Between the Lines*. 2014. 68" × 38".
Calico. Machine pieced, machine quilted, free motion machine stitched text. | Photo: Michael Wicks.

IN THE NEGATIVE SPACE BETWEEN THE STITCHING, YOUR THOUGHTS CAN RUN FREE. THE SEWING MACHINE FEELS LIKE AN EXTENSION OF THE BODY. HAND, FOOT AND EYE WORK TOGETHER, SIMULTANEOUSLY CONTROLLING AND RESPONDING TO THE MOVEMENT OF THE NEEDLE IN A RHYTHM THAT SEEMS TO BE AS NATURAL AND INVOLUNTARY AS YOUR OWN HEARTBEAT, UNTIL THE THREAD FLOWS THROUGH THE SYSTEM LIKE BLOOD. THIS PROCESS, ON ONE LEVEL, IS SLOW AND ALL-ABSORBING. ON ANOTHER, THE HOURS RACE PAST. DECISIONS ARE TAKEN MOMENT BY MOMENT IN A KIND OF WORDLESS DIALOGUE WITH THE MATERIALS DURING WHICH YOUR MIND IS SWEPT CLEAR OF ITS USUAL CLUTTER, EXPOSING A CREATIVE SPACE WHERE IDEAS BUBBLE UP SPONTANEOUSLY. IN THIS STATE OF AWARENESS, EVERYDAY LINEAR TIME SEEMS TO BE SUSPENDED, OR EXPERIENCED IN TERMS OF QUALITY RATHER THAN QUANTITY. YOU MAY BE ASKED HOW LONG A PARTICULAR PIECE OF WORK TOOK TO MAKE AND FIND IT HARD TO GIVE A SATISFACTORY AND ACCURATE ANSWER BECAUSE YOU'RE NOT QUITE SURE AND YOU MAY NOT EVEN CARE. IT'S THE TRANSFORMATIVE ACT OF MAKING THAT IS IMPORTANT: THE PHYSICAL CONNECTION WITH THE TEXTURE OF FABRIC AND THREAD, THE EVOLVING INTERPLAY OF COLOURS AND SHAPES AND THE FASCINATION OF WATCHING A NEW TEXTILE SURFACE EMERGE IN INCREMENTAL STAGES, BUILDING UP GRADUALLY UNTIL A CRITICAL MASS OF STITCHING IS ACHIEVED AND THE WORK IS COMPLETE. IT MAY HAVE STARTED AS LITTLE MORE THAN A VAGUE IDEA, BUT NOW IT EXISTS AS AN ARTEFACT IN ITS OWN RIGHT WITH ITS OWN INDIVIDUAL SET OF CHARACTERISTICS: ITS FEEL, ITS HANDLE, ITS SOFTNESS OR STIFFNESS, ITS ABILITY TO CLOTHE, DECORATE, CONTAIN, WRAP, CONCEAL OR REVEAL. IT CAN BE DRAPED, ROLLED, FOLDED, PLEATED OR CRUMPLED. IT CAN BE SEEN, TOUCHED, TREASURED OR THROWN AWAY. IT IS OUT THERE, NO LONGER YOURS, YET ALWAYS YOURS, MIRRORING IN TANGIBLE FORM THE MAKING PROCESS IN WHICH, PARADOXICALLY, YOU SEEM TO BOTH LOSE AND FIND THE SENSE OF SELF. DOES ALL THIS MATTER TO ANYONE ELSE? SOME PEOPLE SAY THAT PROCESS AND CONTEXT ARE OF LITTLE RELEVANCE AND THAT THE ARTWORK SHOULD BE VIEWED IN ISOLATION. YET WHATEVER ITS MERITS OR DEMERITS, THE TIME AND EFFORT INVOLVED ARE EVIDENT EVEN TO A CASUAL OBSERVER, WHO IS INVITED TO LOOK BENEATH THE SURFACE AND SPECULATE ABOUT HOW AND WHY IT CAME TO BE MADE. SOMETHING IS COMMUNICATED THAT CAN'T BE SEEN OR TOUCHED BUT IS THERE TO BE READ IN THE NEGATIVE SPACE BETWEEN THE LINES OF STITCHING. ©2014

Text from *Following the Thread*

"Stitching can be almost a visceral experience as if the sewing machine were an extension of the body. Hand, foot, and eye work in harmony, simultaneously controlling and responding to the momentum of the needle in a rhythm that comes to feel as natural and involuntary as a heartbeat. A system of belts, shafts, wheels, and discs sends messages like nerves until the thread flows as freely as blood. In this intimate relationship the thread is the raw material to be transformed into an embroidered or quilted design. Thread is everywhere. Across cultures, it accompanies us from birth to death. It is used in ritual and commemoration and as an expression of identity. Thread is dynamic. Thread speaks. Thread connects."

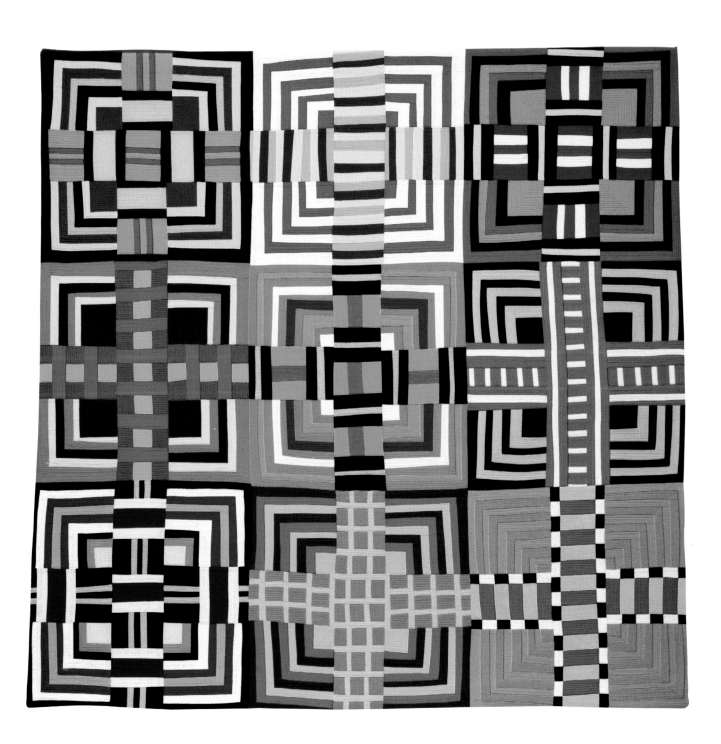

Maria Shell

Alaska, USA.
Dance Party at Tamara's House. 2012. 37" × 37".
Vintage and contemporary commercial fabrics,
hand-dyed cottons. Improvisationally cut, pieced,
machine quilted. | Photo: Chris Arend.

Marianne R. Williamson

Florida, USA.
Playing with the Light. 2013. 38" × 72".
Ice-dyed cotton and silk, paint, ink. Raw edge appliquéd,
free motion quilted. | Photo: Gregory Case.

Hsin-Chen Lin

Tainan City, Taiwan.
Tugging. 2004. 76" × 70".
Cotton. Hand pieced, hand quilted.
Photo: Wu Chung-Yen.

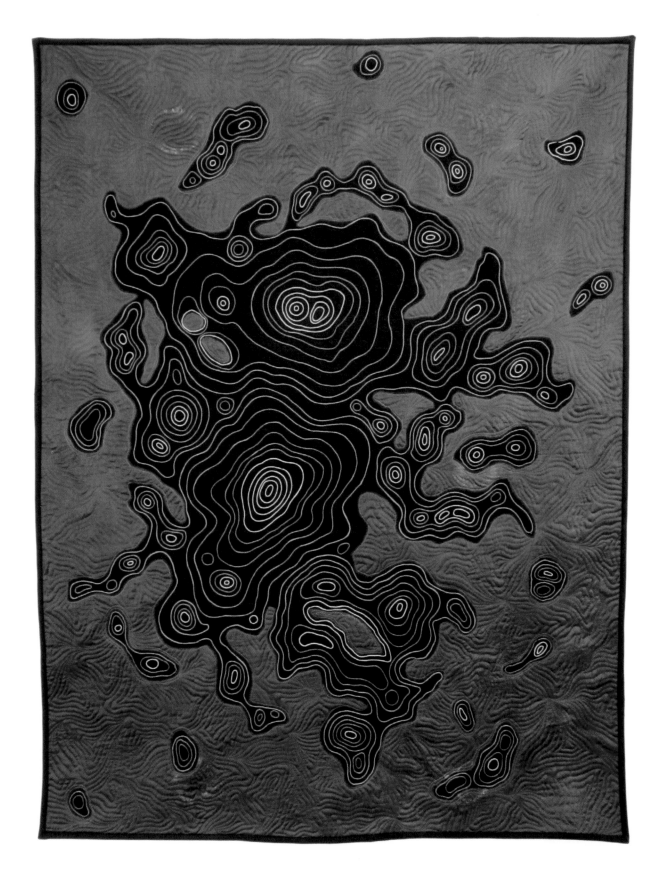

Shea Wilkinson

Nebraska, USA.
Skywalker. 2013. 45" × 33".
Hand-dyed silk, cotton. Machine appliquéd,
free motion quilted.

Judy Kirpich
Maryland, USA.
Circles No. 6. 2011. 61" × 57".
Hand-dyed cottons dyed by Annette
Wink. Machine pieced and quilted.
Photo: Mark Gulesian.

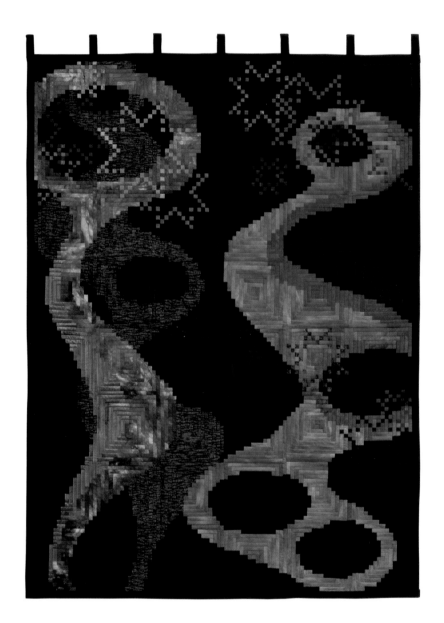

Star Hunter back. 2013.

Emiko Toda Loeb

New York, USA, and Kyoto, Japan.
Star Hunter front. 2013. 82" × 62".
Antique Japanese cotton aizome and hand-dyed, batiked new cotton. Reversible construction where piecing and quilting are done simultaneously. | Photos: D. James Dee.

Charlotte Ziebarth

Colorado, USA.
With Time: Ruins Series #4. 2013. 39" × 40".
Silk, ink, paint. Digital art printed on silk, layered
with painted fabrics, free motion stitched.

Denise L. Roberts
West Virginia, USA.
Sisu #2. 2013. 59" × 59".
Hand-dyed cotton. Machine pieced, machine quilted.
Photo: Richard Roberts.

Bonnie M. Bucknam
Washington, USA.
Tangle. 2010. 88" × 89".
Hand-dyed cotton. Machine pieced and quilted.
Photo: Mark Frey.

Susan Leonard

Pennsylvania, USA.
The Elements. 2013. 24" × 34".
Silk, silk organza. Fused, machine pieced
and stitched. | Photo: John Woodin.

Pat Pauly

New York, USA.
Mummy Bags Influence. 2011. 73" × 80".
Hand-dyed and commercial cotton. Discharged,
painted, dyed, silk screened, pieced.

Helena Scheffer

Beaconsfield, Quebec, Canada.
Spontaneous Combustion. 2010. 55" × 75".
Hand-dyed and commercial cotton and silk.
Collaged, machine quilted.
Photo: Maria Korab-Laskowska.

Dij Pacarro

Florida, USA.
Roman Buildings I-V. 2013. 21" × 30".
Cotton. Pieced, raw edge appliquéd, machine
stitched and quilted.

Betty Ann Guadalupe

Oregon, USA.
Palette of Jeans. 2004 73" × 73".
Blue jeans. Intuitively pieced, long-arm quilted
by Kathy Martin. | Photo: Peter Vilms.

Keiko Ike

Kochi-ken, Japan.
Vision of Blue. 2010. 73" × 74".
Cotton. Machine pieced, appliquéd, quilted.

Thelma McGough

London, UK.
Urban Buzz. 2009. 36" × 78".
Cotton inkjet sheets. Digitally manipulated artist's
photographs, machine pieced and quilted, hand
embroidered. | Photo: Roberto Buzzolan.

Bob Mosier

Texas, USA.
Different Perspectives One. 2013. 12" × 11".
Thread. Thread painted.

Barbara W. Watler

Florida, USA.
Fishing. 2014. 34" × 42".
Organic cotton sateen, poly/cotton,
perle thread. Hand stitched.
Photo: Gerhardt Heidersberger.

Janet Steadman

Washington, USA.
Dream Fields. 2010. 61" × 60".
Hand-dyed cotton. Machine pieced and quilted.
Photo: Michael Stadler.

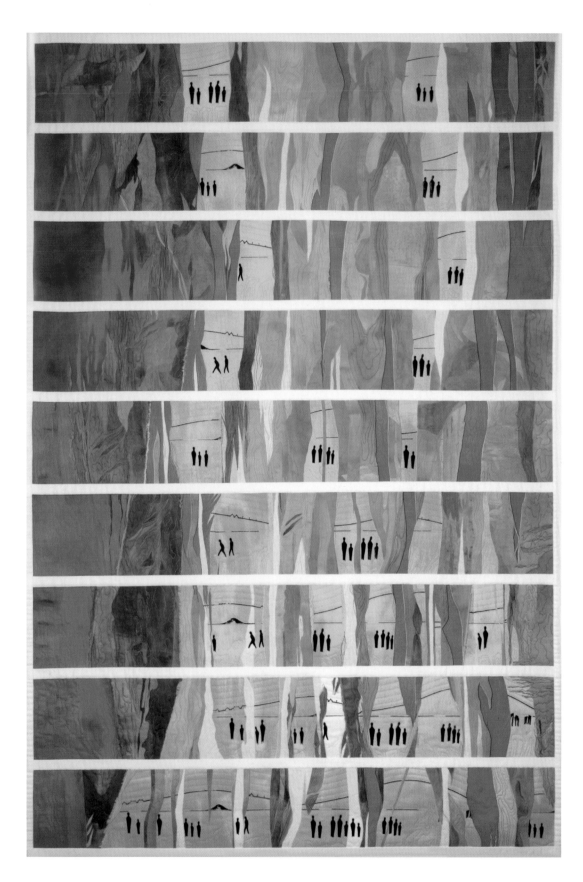

Kathy Unwin

Warwickshire, UK.
Figures in a Landscape. 2009. 64" × 42".
Cotton. Painted, screenprinted, collaged, raw edge
appliquéd, pieced, free motion quilted.

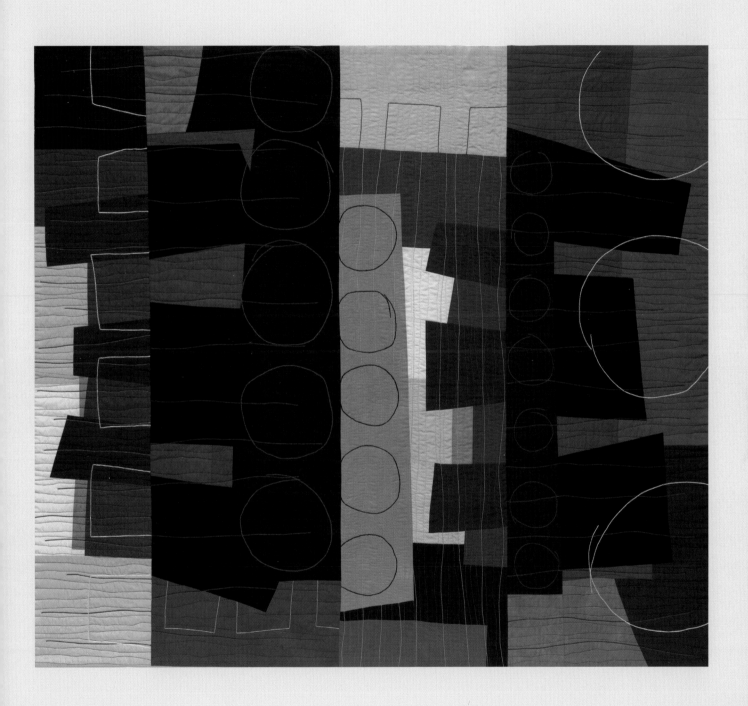

Karen Schulz

Maryland, USA.
Out the In Door. 2013. 58" × 66".
Hand-dyed cotton. Machine pieced,
quilted, couched, hand stitched.
Photo: Gulezian/Quicksilver.

Anne Solomon

Toronto, Ontario, Canada.
Welsh Poppies. 2013. 31" × 32".
Hand-dyed cotton, batiks, silk, organza, ribbon. Appliquéd,
free motion stitched. | Photo: Sylvia Galbraith.

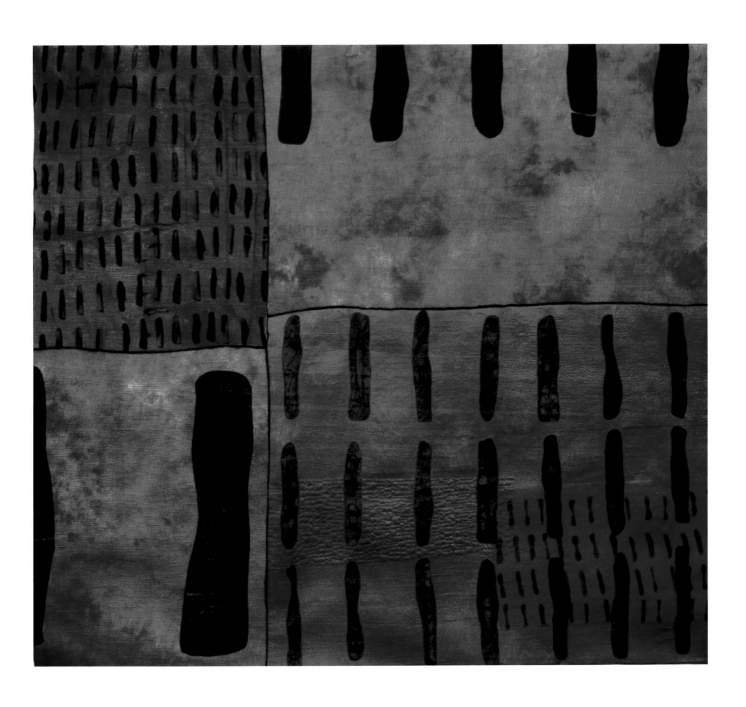

Cecília González Desedamas

Barcelona, Spain.
The Difference. 2012. 72" × 65".
Hand-dyed and -painted silks. Appliquéd and
free motion quilted. | Photo: Pep Izquierdo.

BJ Parady

Illinois, USA.
Lake Cooper. 2007. 49" × 16".
Hand-dyed and -painted silk, ribbon.
Machine quilted, hand embroidered.

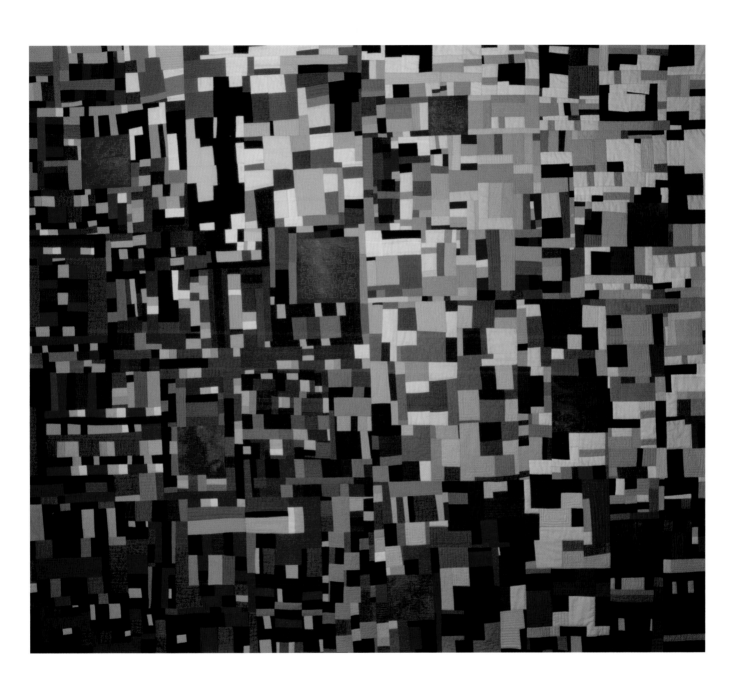

Lauren K. Strach

Michigan, USA.
Hopscotch. 2014. 59" × 68".
Hand-dyed and commercial cotton. Intuitively pieced.
Photo: Michel Marie Rose.

Elsbeth Nusser-Lampe
Freiburg, Germany.
Spring. 2013. 51" × 51".
Hand-dyed cotton, silk, tulle, organza. Collaged,
appliquéd, machine quilted. | Photo: Volker Lampe.

Toni F. Smith

Oregon, USA.
Deconstructed Redwoods. 2014. 33" × 23".
Cotton. Machine pieced and quilted.

Joy Saville

New Jersey, USA.
Karner Blues. 2012. 27" × 63".
Cotton, linen, silk. Pieced, stitched, constructed.
Photo: Taylor Photo.

Cherry Vernon-Harcourt

Essex, UK.
Hunstanton Cliffs. 2014. 48" × 58".
Cotton sateen, dyes. Reconstructed
screenprinting, machine quilted.

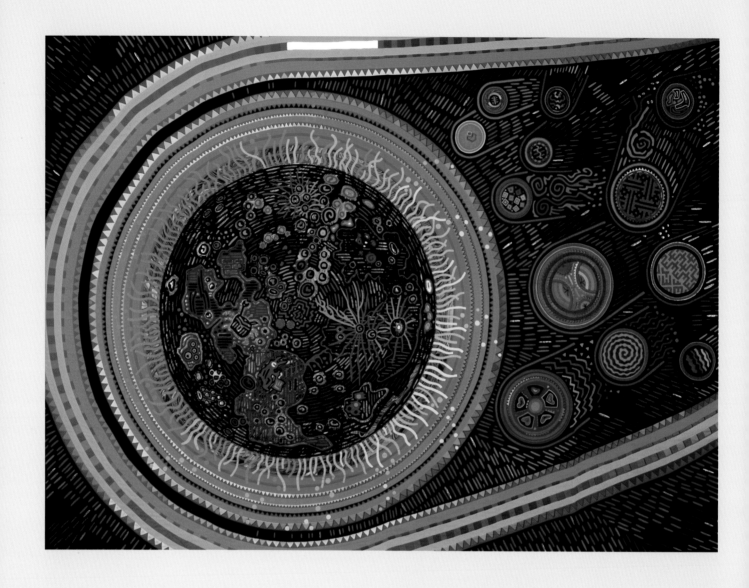

Fumiko Nakayama

Kyoto, Japan

Bold, vibrant color erupts out of the works by Fumiko Nakayama. Complex designs emerge from her continual exploration of novel ways to combine and recombine simple geometric shapes using her reverse appliqué mola techniques. Each piece is a celebration of the beauty of the universe, composed in an amazing arrangement of color and form

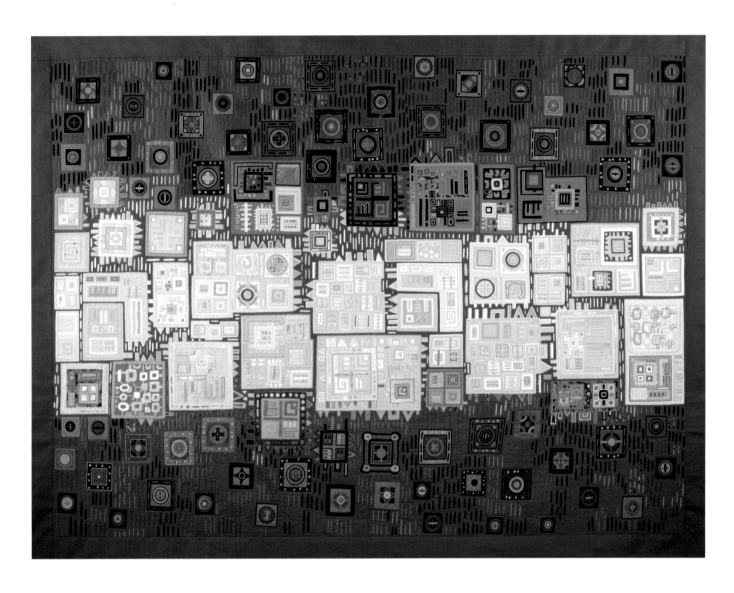

First experiences

My mother and grandmother taught me to sew. The first thing that I sewed was an *otedama*, a Japanese beanbag. I learned Japanese-style painting in grade school. I studied for five years under Shunko Hikita, whose master was Shunkyo Yamamoto. I was planning to become a painter. However, I became interested in fashion, illustration, and embroidery. I had an opportunity to publish a book on embroidery (*Three-dimensional Embroidery*, published by Graphic-sha). That opened up opportunities for me to teach as an embroidery artist.

I first encountered mola reverse appliqué during a visit to the design department of the Asahi Kasei Corporation in 1967. They had only one example of Panamanian mola in their collection. When I first saw it, I was astonished. It was as if an electric current trickled down into me, and I was thrilled with the marvelous technique and colors.

Since I saw that first mola, I have traveled to Panama more than ten times to carefully study the work of the Guna [also spelled Kuna or Cuna] people of Panama, copying their designs to learn as much as I could about traditional mola techniques.

Two years after I started studying mola, I began designing my own original pieces. Now all of my pieces are my own designs. The techniques I use are ones that I have discovered little by little in the process of making mola. It is a bit more complex than making a pieced quilt, because you have to carefully plan the order of construction. This is sort of like solving a puzzle, which I enjoy.

Fabric choices

I don't dye fabric myself, so I have colors dyed for me. I use primarily solid colors, but recently I have been experimenting with printed cotton fabrics from the United States. The fabrics produced in the United States come in a rich variety of designs, and I am attracted to their bold use of color.

I don't find the hand sewing (whip stitching) difficult. However, I recently produced a line of fabrics that are easier to sew through than broadcloth. Needless to say, they are also good for quilting.

ABOVE *Eawase*. 2010 19" × 25". Cotton. Hand reverse appliquéd in mola style, hand embroidered. Photo: Jun Kobayashi.

LEFT *Aoi*. 2011. 19" × 25". Cotton. Hand reverse appliquéd in mola style, hand embroidered. Photo: Jun Kobayashi.

Genji Monogatari

Of all of the mola that I have made, my favorite series is a mola representation of *Genji Monogatari* (The Tale of Genji), which is a very old story. It has been told for more than a thousand years and includes fifty-four *jo* (chapters) of stories. I was not sure how long it would take to complete the entire series of stories in mola, but I wanted to do all of them. This series took me seven years to complete, but I had expected it would take longer.

I started reading the stories in my teens. I have always loved the beautiful depictions of seasonal transitions used throughout the stories. Some of the places described in the stories still bear the same names. The Ishiyamadera Temple that I often visited as a child is said to be where Murasaki Shikibu developed her plan for the story. The temple still retains her room.

Despite the age of this story, the emotions experienced by the characters, particularly the female characters, still resonate with modern women. This makes it an enjoyable read. My favorite character is Rokujo no Miyasudokoro. I find her beauty, intelligence, passion, and dedication appealing.

Color and design

My favorite part of the process is thinking up new designs. Everything I see and hear can become the beginning of a design. I paint as part of my design process, and I try to freely express my reactions to landscape, the universe, flowers, and so on. My works are an attempt to express in colors what I have seen and felt. I follow my intuition.

Geometric composition is my forte. Each of my works has its own theme. While I often use common designs, such as flowers, houses, hearts, and birds for many of my pieces, others are completely abstract, based on simple geometric forms. I regard being able to design in both ways to be a required skill for an artist.

Mola must be designed taking its particular techniques into consideration. If you don't, you will find that more often than not your designs cannot be executed. This sometimes makes the creative process very difficult. However, I will not stop working until a piece is complete. If I am not satisfied, I will change the design or change the colors. Sometimes I will change the embroidery stitches or the mola work. I keep working until I am satisfied.

ABOVE *Geometric*. 2007. 45" × 34". Cotton. Hand reverse appliquéd in mola style, hand embroidered. | Photo: I-jun.

LEFT *Twinkle Forest*. 2008. 68" × 91". Cotton. Hand reverse appliquéd in mola style. | Photo: I-jun.

Yael David-Cohen

London, UK

An exciting mix of fabric and paint characterizes the work of Yael David-Cohen. Slashing brush strokes energize the surface, while the repetition of printed motifs creates a sense of balance. Enigmatic patterns of frames, circles, and spirals, along with tangles of color, hint at mysterious messages just beyond our grasp.

Printmaking

I studied printmaking at St. Martin's School of Art in a postgraduate course. I have combined printmaking with my other artistic activities. For over twenty-five years, I have worked mainly with textiles since I feel this best suits my mode of expression. The use of textiles allows me to create a space whose dimensions I do not know when I start the work. I do not have defined boundaries, cutting, tearing, and sewing the textiles so that the size of the work is only determined on its completion. I work instinctively, responding to the textures and marks on the materials. I continue to display my works without frames, enabling them to appear without borders.

I have been making prints for many years, mainly etchings. When I started working on textiles, I experimented with how I could apply some of my techniques to fiber. This was very exciting for me after printing on paper. I found that each fabric reacts differently to the printing plates. I especially enjoy exploring pattern repetition. For etching on fabric I use printing ink, and for painting on fabric I use acrylics and sometimes industrial paints.

I use printing to create both art quilts and limited edition artist books. The piece shown in the photo of myself is a long work—over four meters—that tells a visual story. This is a piece where the work I do in books and paintings overlaps.

OPPOSITE *Quartet*. 2009. 43" × 57".
Found fabric, scrim, paint, ink. Painted, printed, hand sewn. | Photo: Max Alexander.

Dark Lantern. 2011. 56" × 24".
Found fabric, scrim. Painted, drawn, hand sewn.
Photo: Max Alexander.

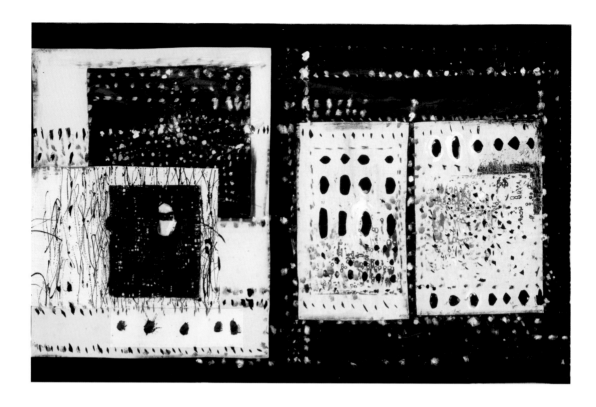

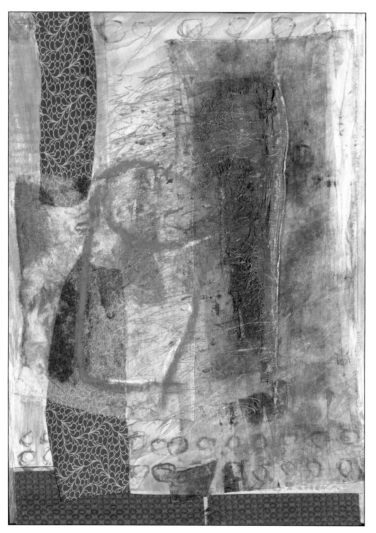

Found textiles

I feel that I have a special relationship with fabric. I especially enjoy its varying textures. For a long time I used various types of paper in my work, such as wallpaper. But I found that the large papers were damaged very easily, so gradually I've moved to using more and more fabrics.

I use found textiles as the idea of giving them a new lease on life is something I enjoy. I take great pleasure in hunting for different textiles, which I then layer, mixing opaque and transparent fabrics to create depth and a three-dimensional effect. I buy remainders of fabric in department stores, and friends who know my work give me discarded textiles. Recently a friend inherited some lace and gave it to me. I am now using this lace in my work.

ABOVE *Perforated Page*. 2011. 34" × 53".
Found fabric, paint, ink. Painted, drawn, hand sewn.
Photo: Max Alexander.

LEFT *Green Glass*. 2009. 51" × 32".
Found fabric, paint, ink. Painted, printed, hand sewn.
Photo: Max Alexander.

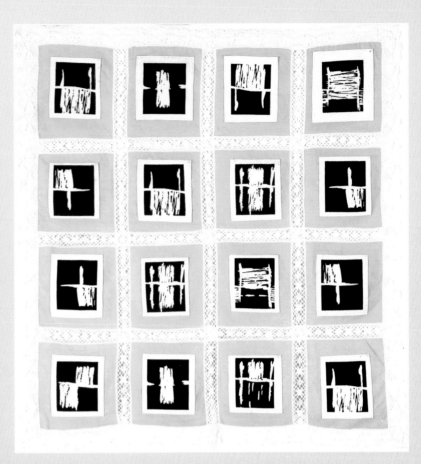

Conversation with myself

My work is concerned with change, order, and disorder. Each of my works represents a conversation that I am having with myself, but which aims to communicate with the viewer. I use frames as a recurring motif because I am interested in the contrast between being inside of a frame and getting out of it.

My work tends toward abstraction but is influenced by natural processes including growth, flowering, withering, and fading. I emphasize the contrasts between dark and light, flow and stagnation, active and passive, transparent and opaque. Often the work is divided using geometrical patterns and represents the process of change from one state to another.

I work with a variety of mixed media, drawing on textiles with pencils, pastels, oil sticks, and acrylic paint. I often print directly onto the material too. This process allows me to "excavate" the layers of color and form that belong to the textiles. I choose my colors depending upon my mood and the subject I am working on. I do not have a particular favorite surface design application, but let myself be inspired by the materials.

Layers and stitching

I work in layers to give depth to the work. This requires stitching. I like to stitch by hand as this allows me to immerse myself in the work. The repetitive act of sewing serves as a form of meditation in contrast to the more spontaneous free expression of painting.

ABOVE *Black & White Story.* 2013. 35" × 33".
Found fabric, lace. Painted, linocut printed, drawn, hand sewn. | Photo: Max Alexander.

LEFT *Whirlpool.* 2013. 54" × 39".
Found fabric, paint, ink. Painted, hand sewn and embroidered. | Photo: Max Alexander.

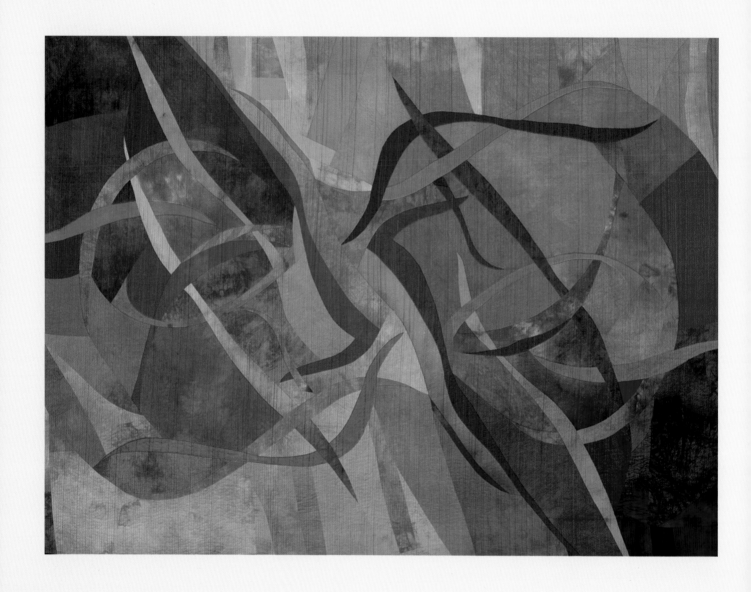

Uta Lenk
Vilsbiburg, Germany

The title of Uta Lenk's series, *Play of Lines*, aptly describes her work. Lenk's art incorporates swooping lines that seem to play across the surface without a care. However, each piece involves meticulous execution of techniques: hand-dyeing fabrics, planning and piecing, and dense quilting. The result is a wide-ranging body of work full of movement and surprise.

Play of Lines

When my son started discovering pens and pencils and making lines at age two and a half, I watched how he chose the different colors and how he drew the lines. It wasn't just scribbling; he seemed to be making deliberate choices about what he was going to do. This was when he was not even talking properly yet!

So I decided that I would like to try to interpret in fabric what he was drawing. My first piece was a free-cut interpretation of his drawing. I did not want to make an exact replica; I worked to turn his inspiration into my own art piece. It was the beginning of a large series, but only some of the pieces in the *Play of Lines* series are based on my son's drawings.

Hand-dyed fabrics

I use fiber reactive dyes, and I dye in my basement. I run a business, a fabric club where every other month members receive a bundle of six fabrics that I have dyed. I always dye a surplus for each color, some of which goes into the stash in my room and the rest into yardage I carry when going to fairs as a vendor.

I have so much fabric in my studio, I don't need to dye for a specific project! Usually I have a design and an idea of what colors I want. Then I go through my boxes and search for just the right shade. Usually I find it. Or I can always change the design.

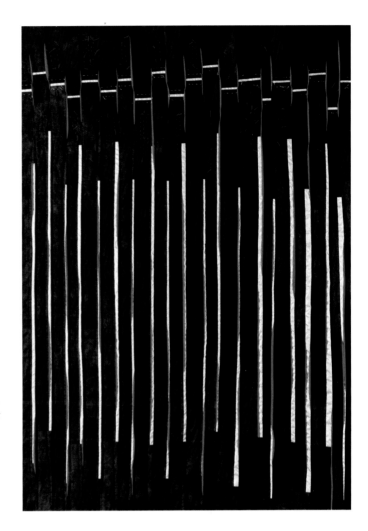

Piecing

I like mastering the technical challenges that come with piecing my complicated designs. I have never been drawn to hand-appliqué, and fusing to me somehow feels like cheating. Plus, I don't like the additional stiffness that comes through the glue layer. I am very much attached to the original feeling of a quilt, the softness. Piecing curved lines is really not that difficult. It's merely a question of proper planning with a pattern. And some patience.

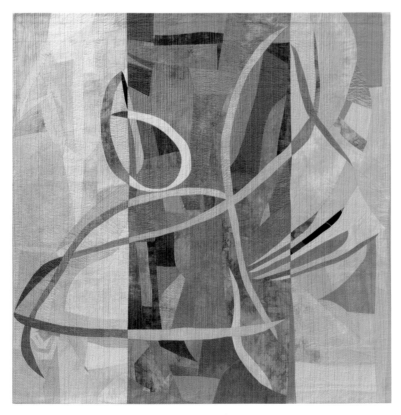

OPPOSITE *Play of Lines XI*. 2008. 59" × 82". Hand-dyed cotton. Machine pieced and quilted. Photo: Andreas Hasak.

ABOVE *Play of Lines XXXVI: Silver Lining*. 2014. 51" × 40". Hand-dyed cotton, reflector fabric. Machine pieced, hand stitched, machine quilted.

LEFT *Play of Lines VIII*. 2008. 73" × 74". Hand-dyed cotton. Machine pieced and quilted. Photo: Thomas Curtze.

Emergencies lead to creativity

Emergency situations are the best for creative impulses. I hate it when they suddenly hit, but they are the ultimate challenge and usually I am pretty happy with the outcome.

Studio Art Quilt Associates (SAQA) had a call for entry for an exhibition entitled *Beyond Comfort*. I planned to create something truly outside my comfort zone: a very narrow, very long quilt that was about three inches wide and over three meters long. My concept was that it would hang down from the ceiling with the rest of it all curling up on the floor. The design was not only beyond my personal comfort zone, but I also hoped to open the juror's eyes about size and form in the arrangement of quilts. The words on *Yellow Line* are sayings, proverbs, and word combinations in German, English, and French that each contain the word for "yellow" in that language.

After having finished *Yellow Line*, I finally closely reread the rules and found out that there was a size restriction. And that my piece didn't fit in. Which really frustrated and annoyed me—why pose such an interesting challenge, and then submit it to size restrictions? It seemed such a contradiction in terms! (Of course it's easier to direct that scorn against somebody else—I should have read the rules more closely in the first place!)

But then I thought about how I had put all this work into the piece, and it certainly wouldn't fit into any rules for other calls for entry. I also listened to my original inner hesitation that a coil on the floor would accumulate too much dust and not be a good experience for the quilt and its appearance in the long term. So I sat down and tried to figure out how I could make it fit into the size restriction. That's how it got folded and woven. It was an emergency thing.

Play of Lines XXXV: Shades of Green. 2014. 47" × 63". Hand-dyed, snow-dyed, and printed cotton. Machine pieced and quilted, hand stitched. | Photo: Andreas Hasak.

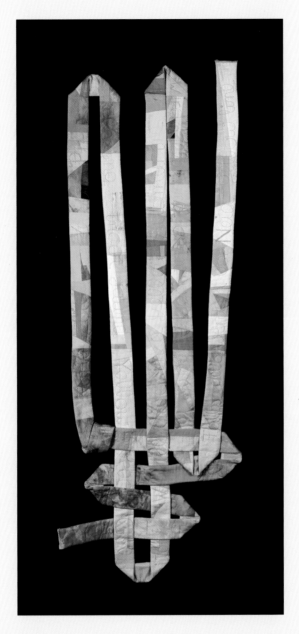

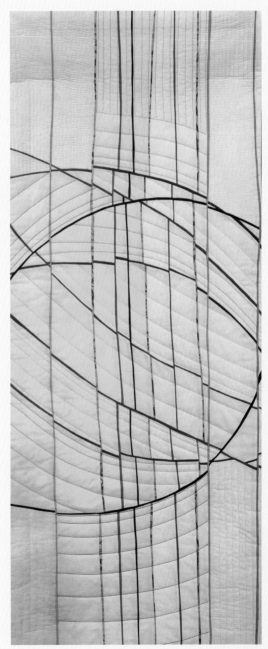

LEFT *Yellow Line*. 2010. 47" × 18".
Hand-dyed and snow-dyed cotton, silk, commercial fabrics. Machine pieced, lettered, and quilted.
Photo: Andreas Hasak.

BELOW *Play of Lines XXIII*. 2010. 45" × 18".
Hand-dyed cotton. Machine pieced and quilted.
Photo: Andreas Hasak.

Quilting decisions and intuition

I have to admit that deciding on the quilting design is absolutely the hardest part for me. Sometimes I fret over it for a very long time and keep putting off getting started. I used horizontal parallel lines for a long time because that was easy, only changing threads every so often for a little bit of color variety. But after a while that didn't satisfy me anymore.

I really like hand quilting. But with my contemporary pieces, traditional hand quilting just doesn't fit. And it takes a long time! So I've started incorporating larger hand stitches, making the whole thing bolder, adding texture.

A lot of my quilting choices are decided intuitively. In fact, much of my work, despite some degree of planning, relies on gut reactions and may be hard to explain. I can't really say that I know what draws me to certain lines and shapes. It's somewhat like book titles—some of them sort of talk to you and call out "read me," whereas others don't even create mild interest.

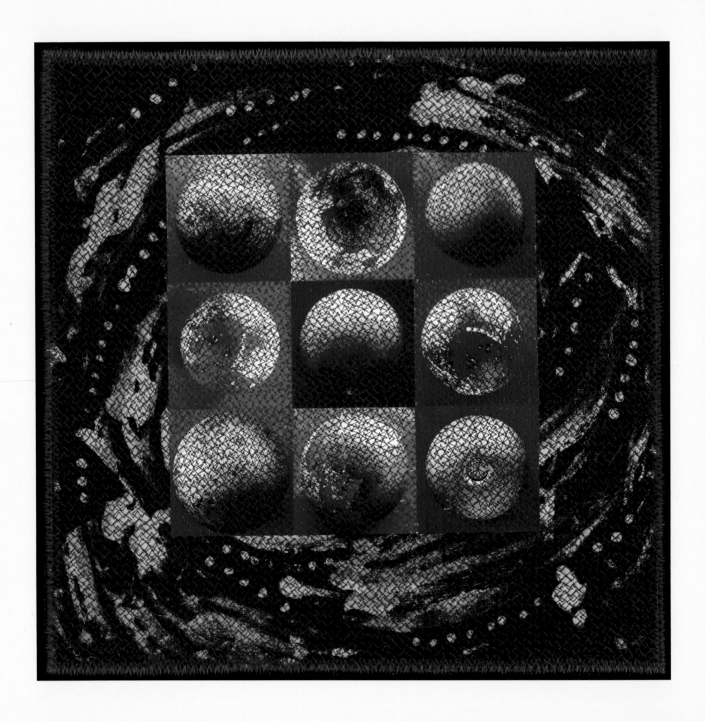

Judy Hooworth

Morisset, New South Wales, Australia

Dora Creek, a small body of water outside Judy Hooworth's home in New South Wales, Australia, has been a primary source of inspiration for her artwork. The circular, repetitive, spiraling lines in much of her work reflect those waters. In recent years, trips to several Asian countries have inspired new directions and design explorations. Color, which was absent for a time, now bursts forth. However, these new designs continue to echo her fascination with circular forms.

Landscape

Just about all of my work is influenced by the landscape, particularly my local environment. There are so many patterns and wonderful color combinations that I can draw upon to create my work. I have an emotional response to what I see around me. I'm never short of inspiration.

I live on Australia's eastern seaboard, about two hours north of Sydney, which has a lovely temperate climate. Australia experiences extremes in temperature and climate, but not usually where I live. Dora Creek begins in the Watagans (part of the Great Dividing Range) and flows down to Lake Macquarie, which is a large saltwater lake that empties into the Pacific Ocean. It is very close by my house, and I walk along the creek a few times each week and birdwatch there too. It's part of my environment, and I'm fascinated by it because it changes so much day by day.

Photography

I take lots of photographs! I've come home from overseas trips with thousands of pictures, and it takes weeks to edit them and file them under different categories. Every time I walk along Dora Creek, I take pictures of the creek from the same east and west viewpoints, patterns in the water, and birds, and anything else I find interesting. Back in the studio I have a practice of drawing a "bird of the day," and I take notes of what I've seen on my walk. I use my photos as references, and I make sketches of my ideas for new work.

Design development

I like abstract linear patterns. I work to particular themes and have a theme in mind before I create the fabrics. I'll make some rough drawings of my ideas as a starting point. Even so, the spontaneity of my approach usually means that something unexpected will happen. I make a lot of fabric and then design directly on the design wall, putting up and taking down until I come up with a composition I'm happy with.

I make changes when new inspiration takes hold. The biggest change was when I moved to where I now live. It was a time of radical change in my life and being in a new environment was inspirational. I had all my fabrics in storage while waiting to build my studio, so it was a perfect opportunity to try something new. I began painting wholecloth quilts and then started creating my own fabrics. I've been making quilts about Dora Creek for the last eleven years, and I have changed techniques a couple of times, usually because I feel I've exhausted that technique or feel it is no longer working for me. I'm excited by change and experimentation, and I would be bored if I just replicated what has been successful in the past.

OPPOSITE *China Souvenir: What Lies Behind #2*. 2014. 11" × 12". Inkjet prints from artist's photographs. Printed, discharged, machine stitched and quilted. | Photo: Garrick Muntz.

Black Water #3. 2010. 19" × 40". Cotton, paint. Hand painted, monoprinted, machine pieced and quilted. Photo: Steve Gonsalves Photographics.

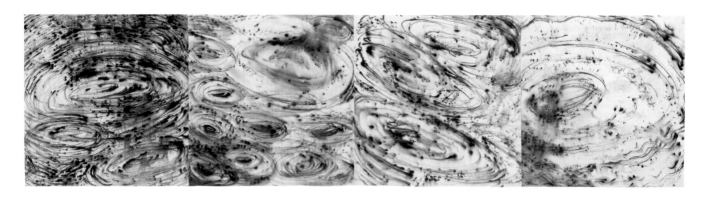

Black Water #32: Into the light diptych. 2012. 34" × 132" each.
Cotton, paint, ink, oil pastel. Hand painted, discharged, drawn, machine
pieced, quilted by Sharon French. | Photo: John Doughty.

Creek Drawing #8. 2012. 48" × 64".
Cotton, paint, ink. Hand painted, machine pieced and quilted.
Photo: Andrew Payne Photographix.

Black Water

The *Black Water* series was made following the death of my husband. The lines are bolder, more visceral, and the palette is fairly dark overall. It's impossible to separate the work from my emotional state. I used a two-inch-wide paintbrush to create the bold lines. Over time my work started to get lighter of its own accord, I guess as my mood lightened. I had gotten to the point where I worked only in black and white. From there I started to add color again, so a much lighter palette felt appropriate, and with that I began to experiment more with finer lines. I took dried plants from my garden, dipped them in ink and used them like a brush. I also drew with crayon and pencils onto the surface of the fabric.

Silk Road

My new series is called *Detour via the Silk Road*, and I've been exploring some different techniques. I took a lot of photos on my travels in 2012 and 2013 to Russia, China, and Central Asia. I particularly like circles. Anything with a circular motif caught my eye. Manhole covers were a favorite. I edited the photos, cropped them, and printed them out, then reorganized the pictures to create new designs. These were stitched together and mounted on fabric I'd created, and then each piece was extensively stitched through all the layers. I've also started creating interpretations of traditional embroidery and tile designs, using deconstructed screen printing techniques. I draw directly onto the screen with water soluble crayons and make monoprints. I don't know yet just where this new change will lead, but I'm excited about the journey.

Creek Drawing #9. 2013. 34" × 67".
Cotton, paint, ink. Hand painted, machine pieced and quilted.
Photo: Andrew Payne Photographix.

Black Water #33. 2012. 37" × 32".
Cotton, paint, ink, oil pastel, crayon. Hand painted, monoprinted, discharged, drawn, machine quilted by Sharon French.

Els van Baarle

Dreischor, the Netherlands

A love of old walls and the language of symbols is evident in the work of Els van Baarle. Subtle, nuanced colors support exploration of layers of indecipherable writing and maps. Thousands of envelopes are stitched together to show how we are all interconnected, yet always alone.

Indonesia and batik

Indonesia was a Dutch colony until 1946, and there was a big Indonesian influence on the Netherlands through trade. I started using wax during my education as a textile teacher. It was in the 1970s, and batik was popular, especially for things such as skirts with large flowers.

Batik became my thesis. After school I had lessons from an Indonesian teacher. He taught me to work with the traditional tjaps, tjanting, and naphthol dyes. The tools are originally from Indonesia. In the early days, before 1850, every design was hand drawn in wax on the fabric by women using the tjanting. Around 1850, the copper stamp was invented. The work was still laborious because it required using a mirror image as the fabric was worked first on the front and then later on the back with the mirror stamp. The stamped designs were done by men.

I fell in love with batik: the smell of the wax, the dyes, and the tools. I loved it all. And it was a wonder to me how I could transform fabric using many layers of wax and dyes to get so many nuances, a myriad of colors. I used natural fabrics: linen, cotton, silk, and Procion reactive dyes, since the naphthol dyes are no longer considered safe.

Nowadays, I also work a lot on paper. I started using paper by happy accident. When I was working on cloth, I tested the colors on paper and I wiped up the excess dye from on top of the wax. The colors were so brilliant on the paper that I now work side-by-side, paper and fabric. The colors will match, but it is not exactly the same, again nuanced colors. For me that is very interesting. I like them both.

New tools

I have worked for about twenty years in various schools and colleges, giving art lessons. I usually have a very low budget for buying materials. That has made me very creative in finding inexpensive ways of working with my students.

You can find many things around the house that you can use with wax or paint. I look for things with my eyes and hands. I have to feel the textures to know what I can do with it. A piece of wood, covered with strong double-sided tape can hold matches, buttons, pieces of inner tube, etc. I even have printed with foods, like spaghetti and rice.

OPPOSITE *News IV*. 2008. 60" × 32".
Silk, wax, dye. Dyed, discharged, printed with old newspaper, stitched. | Photo: Joop van Houdt.

Counting the Days II. 2013. 40" × 20" each.
Cotton, wax, dye, paint. Dyed, painted, silk screened, stitched. | Photo: Joop van Houdt.

Inspiration photos

Taking photos is my second love. It certainly is connected to my textile work, but I never work with a photo next to me to translate it into cloth. I am drawn to repeating patterns and to the textures of old things. The textures on old walls can inspire the way I handle wax and dye to make an interesting surface.

I see the beauty in the details. You do not have to travel to the other side of the world to see interesting colors and textures. When I take photos, I use the camera as a tool to look for interesting compositions. I take many images from slightly different angles or positions.

ABOVE *Counting the Days III*. 2014. 24" × 14". Antique pillow cover. Dyed, silk screened, stitched. Photo: Joop van Houdt.

LEFT *A Quiet Place III*. 2014. 72" × 80". Silk organza. Batiked, discharged, dyed, silk screened.

___

OPPOSITE

LEFT *Letters from a Friend II*. 2014. 107" × 90". Used envelopes, wax. Silk screened, waxed, stitched. Photo: Joop van Houdt.

RIGHT *You Are Here I*. 2012. 107" × 35". Cotton, paper. Batik, silk screened, stitched. Photo: Joop van Houdt.

Themes

All my work has to do with time passing, the wear and tear of time. I can work on a theme for years. One work leads to another; I always have many more ideas than I can realize. I also love the continuation of a series. I usually choose my colors to go with my themes. For instance, I worked on the theme of Pompeii for a long time. I can mix that special red dye color with my eyes closed. The turquoise I use was also from the Pompeii frescoes. My color choices have changed over the years. When I see work from twenty years ago, it seems very light colored, almost pastel.

In every village or city you see these signboards: *You Are Here*. The series *You Are Here* also has a symbolic meaning for me: Where is your place in the world? In your family? Does it change over the years?

The series *Letters from a Friend* is a tribute to the friendship I and my husband had with Henk Wakkee. He was a schoolteacher who collected stamps and also the used envelopes. Many people he knew saved mail to give him the envelopes. When he died, his wife told me she wanted to throw away his collection of several thousand envelopes. I knew immediately that I wanted to work with these papers. Creating this series, working with his envelopes, has been a beautiful way of mourning his death.

You are here
You are here

149

Paula Kovarik

Memphis, Tennessee, USA

150

A strong, linear quality in Paula Kovarik's work reflects her training as a graphic designer. Her early work is filled with colorful, playful symbols and quirky lines that randomly wander across the surface. Recent pieces are visually more organized, as they are designed to convey serious political statements reflecting her concerns about the environment.

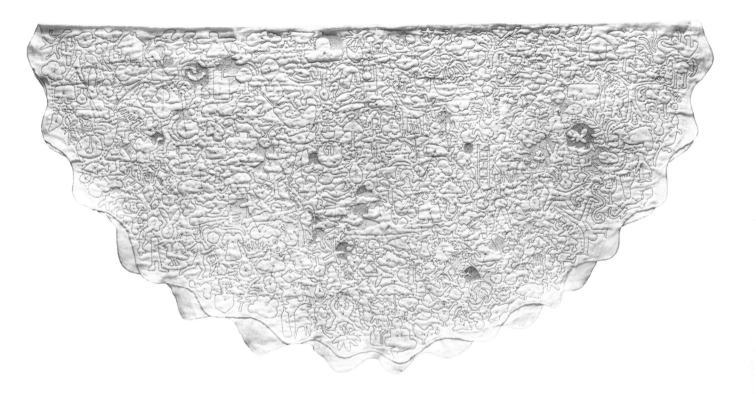

Looking at clouds

Memory's Playground is a study of the way we remember things and the way we imagine them. The idea started when I was playing a game with a group of children. We were looking at clouds and imagining them as dragons or dogs or rocket ships. I chose this tablecloth for its wavy edging and playful form.

I stitched a puzzle of odd images that connect in mysterious ways. Just as our brains connect experiences and ideas, colored threads jump from one image to the next without logic. The profile of a face might be tied to a whale and then to a ladder and then to a bird—as if we are on a little memory walk on the beach. The threads hop from one item to the next and are also tied to each other with small hand-tied knots just as we try to lock in our memories and ideas.

OPPOSITE *Same but not*. 2011. 39" × 42".
Cotton. Free motion quilted, hand stitched.
Photo: Allen Mims.

Memory's Playground. 2014. 27" × 54".
Found cotton tablecloth. Free motion quilted, hand stitched.
Photo: Allen Mims.

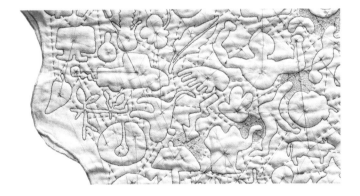

Dreams and insomnia

My dreams inform my work. The quality of those thoughts that come just before sleeping or waking is most mysterious to me. Why am I thinking about something that happened forty years ago? Why do mental images coalesce and evolve? How does the mind sort the input overload? Insomnia can thwart or feed my ideas.

The *Insomnia* pieces are stitched on old, stained pillow shams. At the time, both my husband and I were experiencing difficulty sleeping, and we would compare notes about what was keeping us up at night and which tactics we tried to finally sleep. I tried counting, so there are little counting symbols on the *Hers* side. He tried getting up and walking around, so there is a figure sleepwalking on the *His* piece. Both pieces have stitching that represents the way our minds repeat thoughts over and over again: the threads that hang off the bottom of the *His* piece are simply that—thoughts that linger, dangle, and disappear.

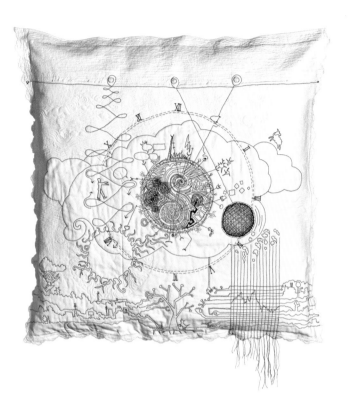

Recycling: *Round and Round It Goes*

I like to use recycled linens. The choice of fabric affects the final composition in many ways. I am drawn to fabric that has been used, because it evokes a sense of history and evolution. I like the idea that people have talked to each other while dining on a tablecloth, that their hands have caressed or stained or torn the cloth over time. It is also a symbol of consumption (eating and drinking), and that's what we are doing with our natural resources.

I set out to convey a sense of order *and* chaos in this piece. I wanted it to be beautiful *and* awful. From the spiral underpinning (representative of DNA, growth, and our galaxy)

ABOVE LEFT *Insomnia: His*. 2014. 28" × 28". Found cotton pillow sham. Free motion quilted, hand stitched. | Photo: Allen Mims.

ABOVE RIGHT *Insomnia: Hers*. 2014. 28" × 28". Found cotton pillow sham. Free motion quilted, hand stitched. | Photo: Allen Mims.

RIGHT *City*. 2008. 41" × 38". Hand-dyed and commercial cotton. Free motion quilted, hand stitched.

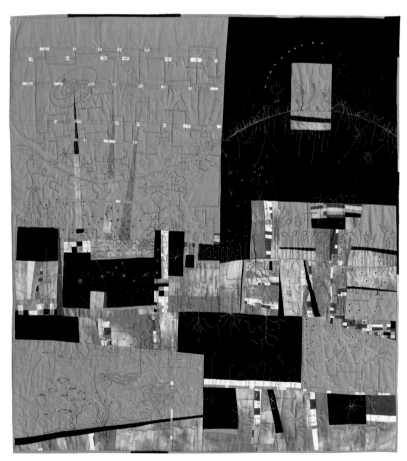

I established a negative side and a positive side to create a balance and counterpoint to the narrative of a threatened Earth. I started with the ocean and the city in the center of the piece to represent the engineered and natural elements of our world. With serious threats to both, specific images were chosen for their positive or negative implications: changing seasons, migrating birds, a nuclear power plant.

Round and round it goes.
2013. 54" circle.
Repurposed cotton tablecloth.
Free motion quilted.
Photo: Allen Mims.

Successes and disasters

When a piece is going well, I am breathless: eager to stitch, eager to be present, and loathe to leave the studio. When I am stuck, I have to walk away. I often pin a piece on my design board and sneak glances at it from time to time. I may turn it upside down or cover half of it with black or white fabric. Sometimes I can see what went wrong; I can find a way back into it. Other times I get out my trusty rotary cutter and slice it up. I once had an art teacher who said that within each bad painting there is a masterpiece. I strive to find a successful part of each disaster.

Sheila Frampton-Cooper

Mallemort, France

Intuitive, improvisational, free-flowing designs characterize Sheila Frampton-Cooper's art. Boldly colored, amorphous shapes dance across the surfaces of her designs. Dense quilting covers the works, adding a subtle layer of emphasis and contrast. Frampton-Cooper invites you to relax and have fun as you enter into her vibrant universe.

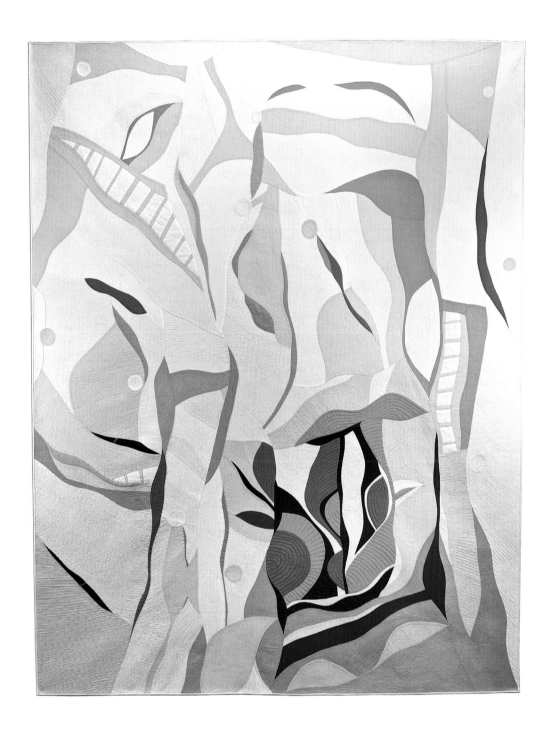

Doodling and improvisation

I think doodling is misunderstood and not viewed seriously. I'm not really crazy about the word "doodling" for that reason. Doodling is a way of drawing when you are totally free and designs just flow from you without worrying or being too fussy about it. I feel this is an invaluable asset to my work as an artist.

I construct as I design. I do not put everything up on the design wall, move it around until I like it, and then sew it all together. I commit to each section as I am creating, by sewing it together and having no idea whatsoever of what will be next to it.

I primarily use my own hand-dyed fabrics. Using hand-dyed fabric affects my work by giving me control of the subtle changes in value that I require, and I aim for bright, saturated colors. I typically dye five to seven values of each color that I'm using. I aim to create the darkest darks of each color and dye at least two yards of each of those.

Piecing

I piece because I love the challenge of engineering a complex composition. It is a major challenge to create a work designed with seams from curved pieced sections. I create the different sections separately, and then I have to put them together. Often this requires a very long and challenging seam.

I may want certain shapes to line up to create another shape, but I do not use pins. I will make a few marks with a white pencil, then I take a deep breath and make it happen! There is a seam in one of my quilts, *The Arrival*, which was crazy. I needed all of these shapes to be aligned, and it had a big curve. When you sew curves without pinning, the fabric will shift so you have to anticipate that in advance. Even then it's hard. This excites and challenges me, and that's good for my brain.

Quilting

I never, never mark my quilts or plan my quilting in advance. I make each decision when I get to a particular section. There are times when a straight line is what calls to me; other times I do a combination of curves.

I see the quilting as movement and energy, directing the eye in a subtle way. I feel that there's great impact in the little—some might think invisible—aspects of quilting. The flow of the lines and shapes of the quilting is very important and something I give a lot of attention to. Of course this could be as simple as echoing the shape but with slight variations. This is one reason I like to closely match my thread color to the fabrics, because I just want the viewer to see the movement.

ABOVE *Red Dragon*. 2012. 38" × 36".
Hand-dyed cotton. Pieced, free motion quilted.

LEFT *Venus in the Garden*. 2013. 63" × 63".
Hand-dyed cotton. Pieced, free motion quilted.

My artistic background includes painting with oils, acrylics, and watercolors. I often use thread and play with the colors as if I were mixing paint. I quilt quite densely, and I like to create the type of texture that I would get if it were a painting. I may want to darken an area just a bit, or lighten it. However, I find that it's always easier to lighten using thread than to darken.

For *Venus*, I chose to quilt in a more painterly manner. For example, for two areas that were touching where the values were different, I used a lighter value of the thread, matching the thread color to the lighter fabric, when stitching on the darker fabric. And I reversed this for the lighter fabric by matching the thread color of the darker fabric and using a darker value thread. The effect was to melt those two shapes together in a subtle way.

If change is necessary

If I'm just beginning, just putting the first few fabrics together, and I don't like it, I will cut it in some way, restructure, and add something else in or put that piece

or section to the side. Once I'm deep in the middle of a piece, I never have issues. If I get to a point where I do not know what to do next, then I just sit back and wait for the solution to dawn on me. I may have a serious construction challenge, but I never put everything together until I'm at peace with the way it looks.

I love creating larger scale, very graphic pieces, because I have more space to play. To be honest, I never know where it's going to go. I don't set out to do any certain thing; it just happens.

ABOVE *A View from Above*. 2011. 63" × 40".
Cotton. Pieced, free motion quilted.

LEFT *The Beach*. 2014. 41" × 24".
Hand-dyed cotton. Pieced, free motion quilted.

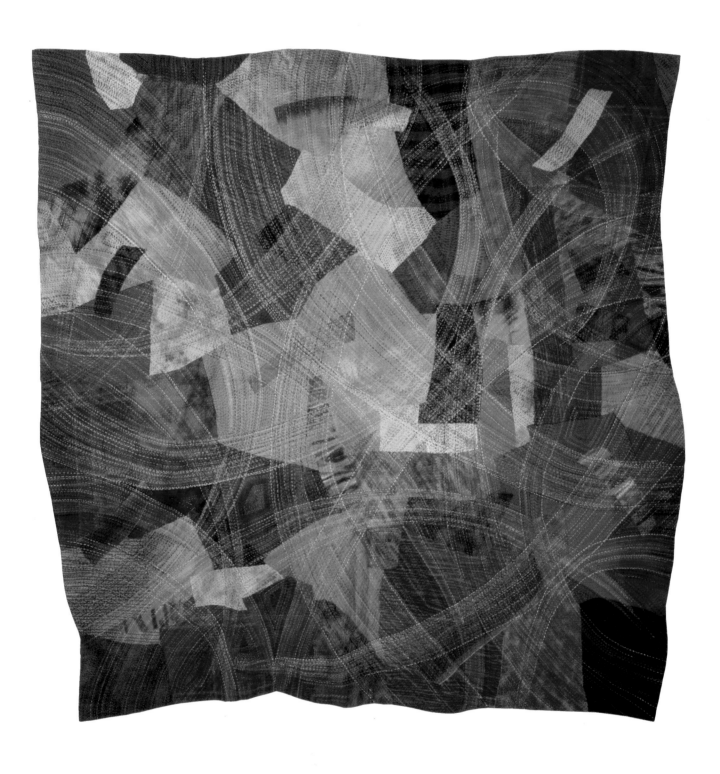

Takako Ishinami

Yamaguchi, Japan.
Where to Autumn. 2007. 78" × 78".
Cotton. Hand appliquéd, sashiko stitched.

Judy Gaynes Sebastian

Massachusetts, USA.
Orange Variation 1. 2008. 37" × 24".
Hand-dyed cotton and silk, commercial cotton and silk,
ultrasuede. Machine appliquéd. | Photo: Orleans Camera.

Roxane Lessa

North Carolina, USA.
Energy #2. 2012. 16" × 20".
Cotton, paintsticks. Fused,
machine quilted, drawn.

Susan Hotchkis
Guernsey, UK.
Fragment. 2013. 41" × 20".
Synthetic voile, cotton, paper. Paper lamination,
free motion stitched, heat distressed.

Cindy Grisdela
Virginia, USA.
Red Totem. 2010. 42" × 20".
Hand-dyed cotton. Improvisationally pieced,
free motion quilted. | Photo: Gregory R. Staley.

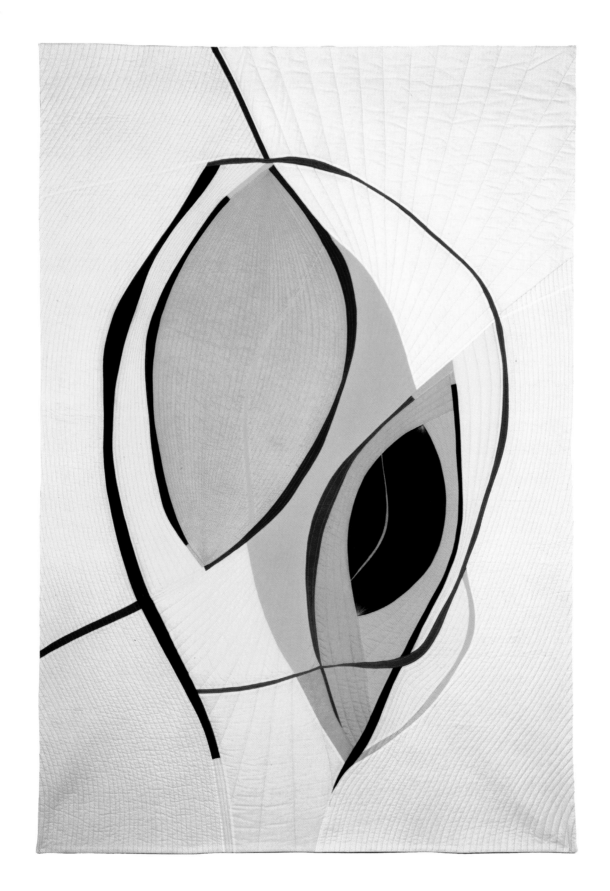

Valerie Maser-Flanagan

Massachusetts, USA.
Chrysalises #2. 2011. 68" × 46".
Hand-dyed cotton. Machine pieced and quilted.
Photo: Joe Ofria.

Maya Chaimavich

Ramat Gan, Israel.
The Tender Grape. 2014. 51" × 51".
Recycled fabrics. Fused, free motion machine
quilted. | Photo: Moti Chaimovich.

Yvonne Kervinen

Osthammar, Sweden.
Urban Landscape. 2014. 51" × 40".
Cotton, paint. Raw edge appliquéd, painted,
printed, free motion machine quilted.

Gail Ingraham

Michigan, USA.
Circles and Squares Number 2. 2014. 27" × 32".
Hand-dyed and sun-bleached cotton. Appliquéd,
machine quilted. | Photo: Andy LePere, Kensho Studio.

Geri deGruy

Colorado, USA.
Bounty. 2014. 24" × 22".
Cotton. Raw edge appliquéd, free-motion stitched.

Paulette Landers

Oregon, USA.
Fissures 1. 2014. 26" × 40".
Hand-dyed cotton and silk, paint. Dyed,
painted, raw edge appliquéd, stenciled,
monoprinted, free motion stitched.

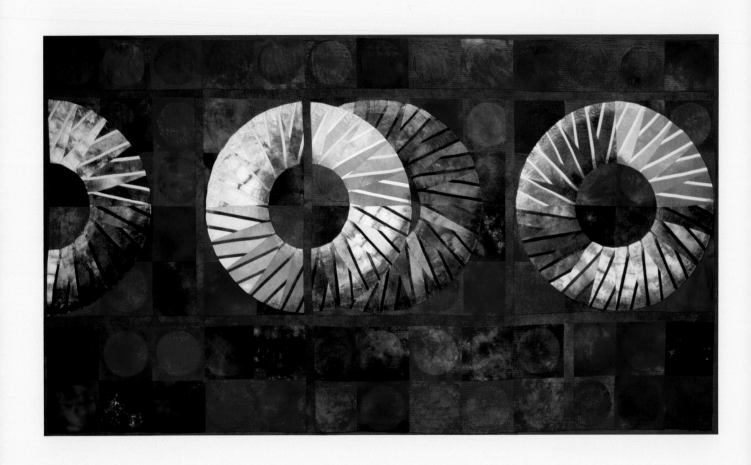

Lyric Montgomery Kinard

North Carolina, USA.
Progress. 2010. 54" × 98".
Hand-dyed cotton. Dyed, pieced,
stitched, painted.

Tara Faughnan

California, USA.
House Top Quilt. 2013. 55" × 55".
Cotton, polyester. Machine sewn and quilted.

Jean M. Sredl

Illinois, USA.
A Time in Stitch. 2014. 45" × 41".
Hand-dyed silk, linen, cotton, and gauze, commercial
batiks, hand-dyed and commercial yarns, paint, ribbons.
Dyed, painted, free motion stitched and embroidered,
hand stitched, hand embroidered.

Domique Arlot

Lyon, France.
The Gold Leaf. 2014. 51" × 27".
Silk, organza, synthetics, paint. Painted, hand appliquéd,
hand and machine embroidered and quilted.

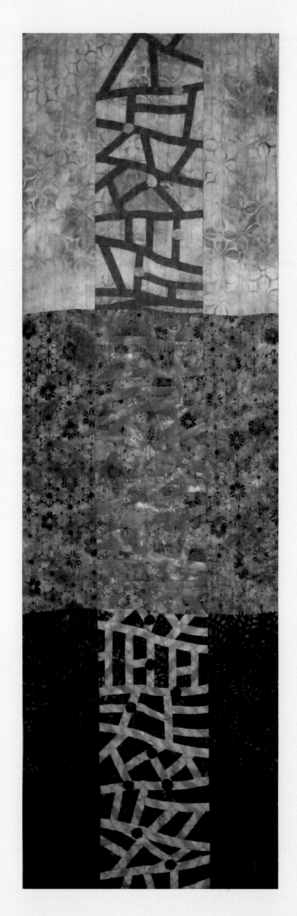

Elena Folomeva
St. Petersburg, Russia.
Interrelation. 2014. 51" × 15".
Cotton. Free hand patchwork, yo-yos.

Grace Harbin Wever

Alabama, USA.
Way of the Whirlwind. 2010. 34" × 29".
Hand-dyed cotton, silk, synthetics, metallic silk.
Collaged, free motion stitched.
Photo: Michael Arterburn.

Georgia French

Oregon, USA.
FractuRED, *TextuRED*, *RED*. 2013. 30" × 24".
Cotton, silk, merino wool roving, yarn. Fused,
felted, hand embroidered, machine quilted.
Photo: John Waller, Imaging by Fox.

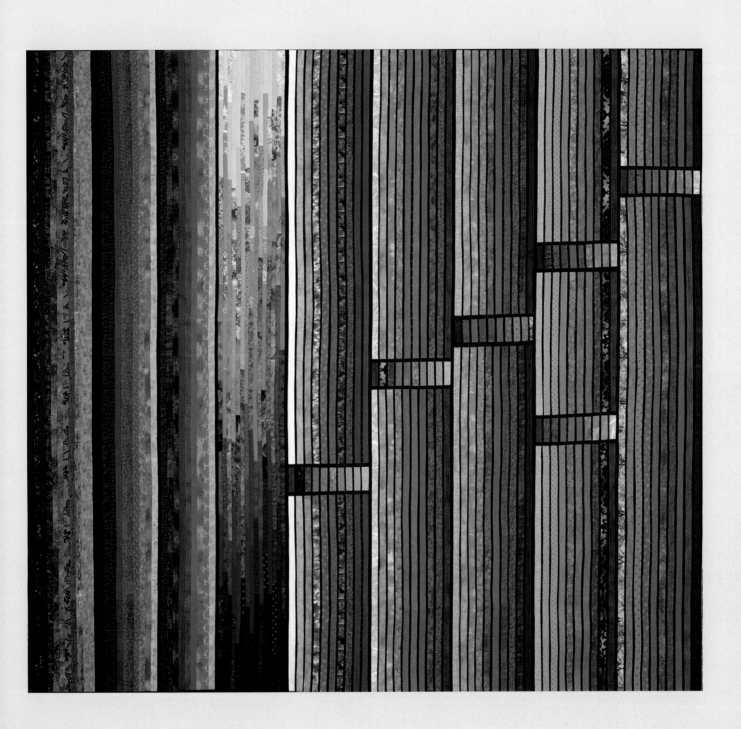

Ann Brauer
Massachusetts, USA.
Modern Red. 2014. 94" × 106".
Cotton. Pieced, free motion quilted.
Photo: John Polak.

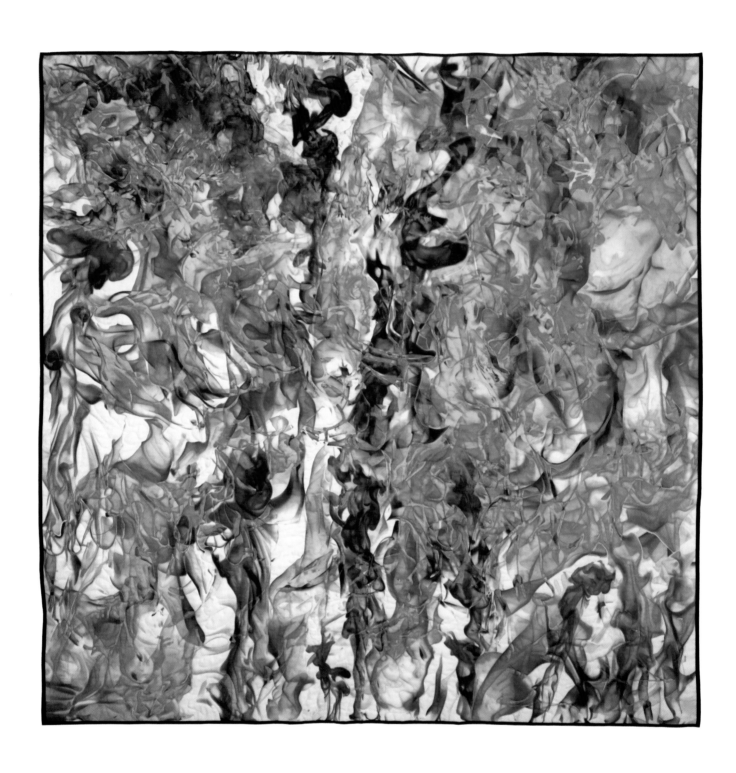

Dan Olfe

California, USA.
Texture Experiment #23. 2012. 57" × 57".
Digitally printed polyester wholecloth. Digitally
printed from 40 flame photographs, machine quilted.

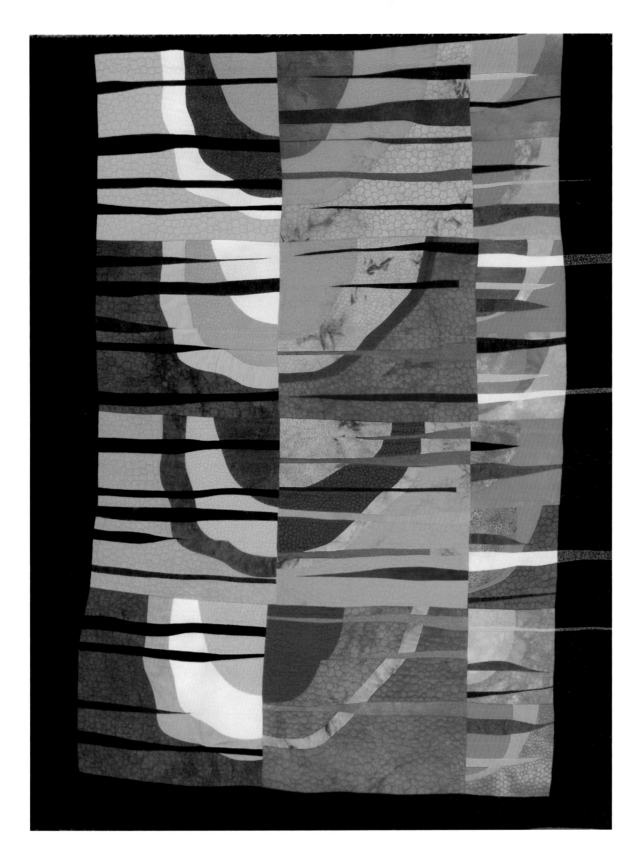

Linda Frost

Kansas, USA.
Geode Slices. 2009. 74" × 56".
Commercial, painted, and hand-dyed cotton.
Machine pieced and quilted, hand quilted.

Bonnie J. Smith

California, USA.
View from Above. 2009. 49" × 41".
Hand-dyed and commercial cotton.
Photography, machine appliquéd, and stitched.
Photo: Luke Mulks.

Andrea Limmer
Virginia, USA.
Maelstrom. 2010. 38" × 32".
Cotton, dye, paint. Screenprinted, painted, machine
appliquéd and quilted. | Photo: Greg Staley.

Elena Stokes

New Jersey, USA.
Infinity. 2014. 43" × 67".
Repurposed silks, discarded saris.
Collaged, fused, machine quilted.

Virginia A. Spiegel

Illinois, USA.
Shagbark 2. 2012. 23" × 36".
Upholstery fabric samples, paint. Machine stitched.
Photo: Deidre Adams.

Daren Pitts Redman
Indiana, USA.
Black and White. 2010. 38" × 42".
Cotton. Machine pieced, machine quilted.
Photo: F. David Redman.

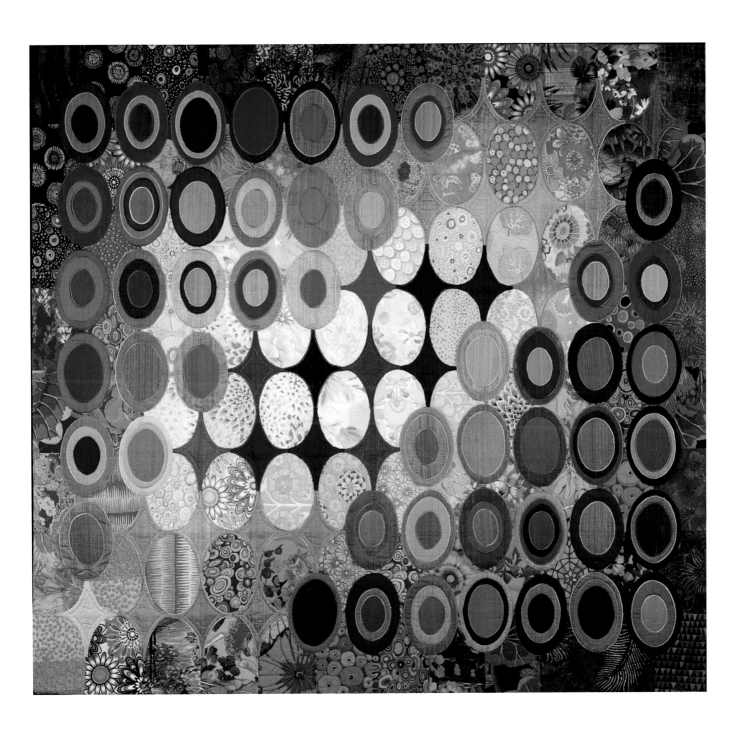

Louisa L. Smith

Colorado, USA.
Ova Nova. 2012. 42" × 45".
Hand-dyed and commercial silks. Dyed, machine pieced,
appliquéd, and quilted. | Photo: Ken Sanville.

Katriina Flensburg

Storvreta, Sweden.
Misty 1-3 triptych. 2011. 30" × 31" each.
Cotton. Dyed, monoprinted, painted, hand
stitched, machine quilted.

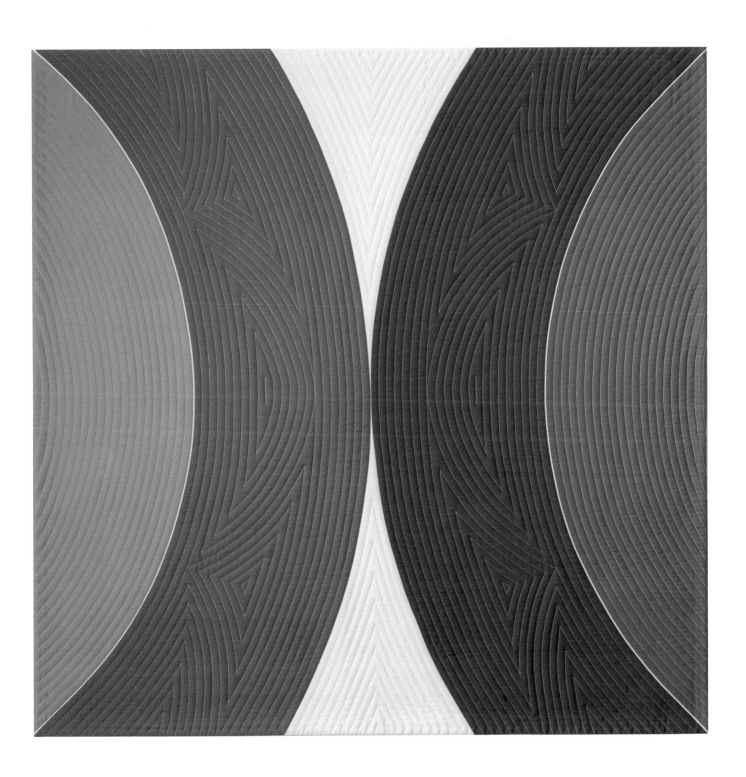

Colleen Wootton

Washington, USA.
2+2. 2012. 41" × 41".
Organic cotton sateen. Digitally printed, stitched.
Photo: Trevor Pearson Photography.

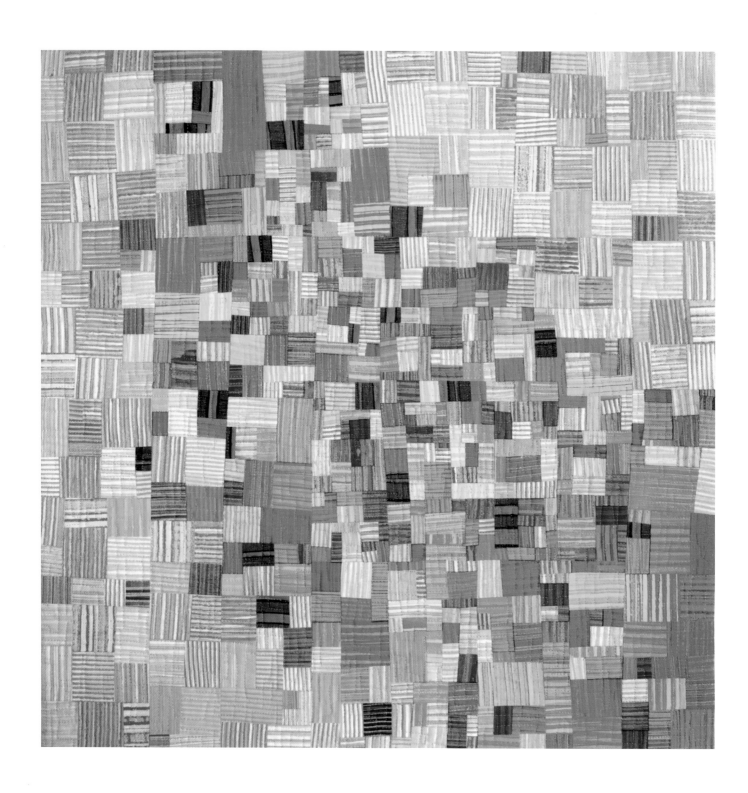

Diane Melms

Alaska, USA.
Fresh Salsa. 2011. 25" × 25".
Hand-dyed and -painted cotton. Dyed,
monoprinted, machine pieced and quilted.

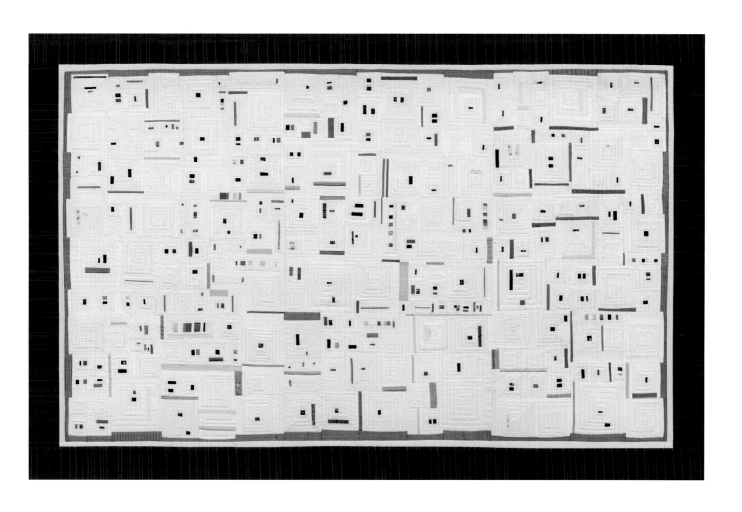

Cynthia L. Vogt

Washington, USA.
Ishi-Datami. 2008. 54" × 34".
Dupioni silk, kimono remnants, hand-loomed textiles,
commercial cottons. Pieced, free motion machine quilted.
Photo: John Warters.

Lisa Call
Colorado, USA.
Structures #148. 2013. 25" × 74".
Cotton, dye. Freehand cut, machine
pieced and quilted.

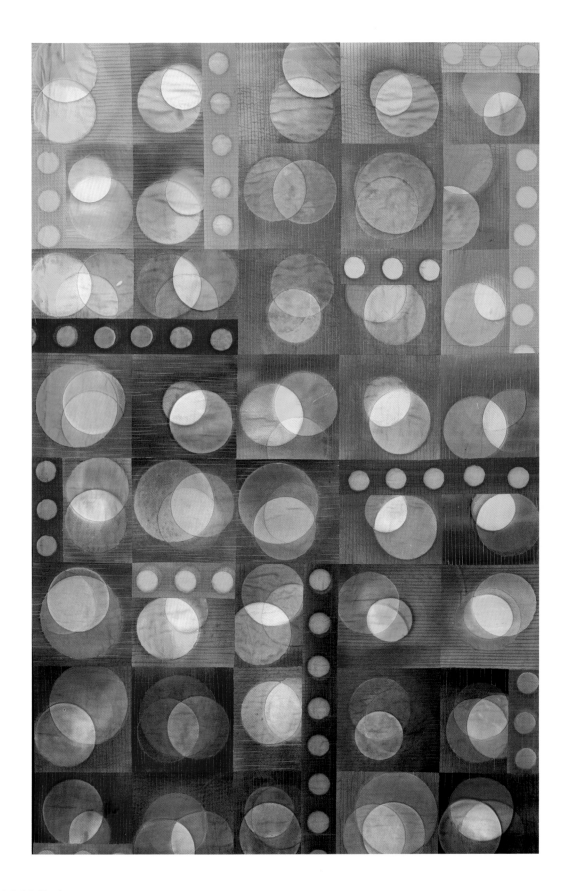

Vicki Carlson

Colorado, USA.
Worlds Apart. 2011. 58" × 36".
Cotton, paint. Solar printed, machine pieced and
quilted. | Photo: Ken Sanville.

Catherine Kleeman

Maryland, USA.
Circular Reasoning. 2013. 33" × 68".
Hand-dyed and -painted cotton. Screen printed, monoprinted, batik,
stamped, painted, machine appliquéd, machine stitched and quilted.

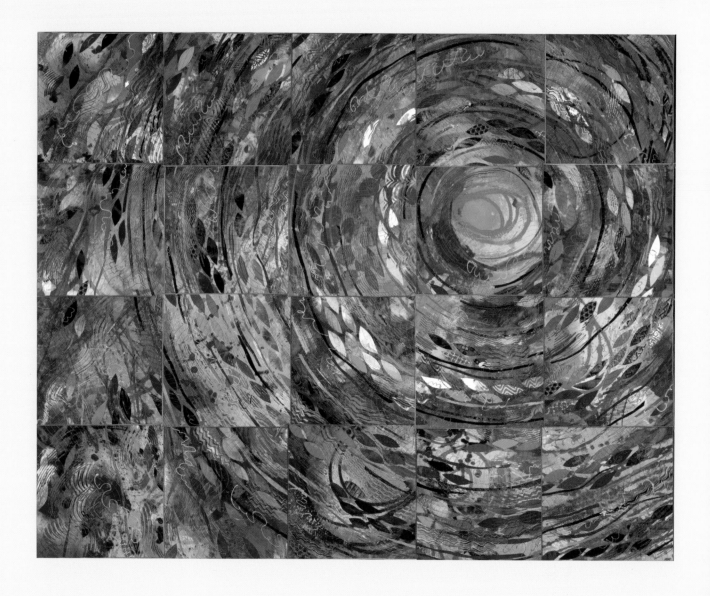

Sue Benner
Dallas, Texas, USA

Complex, intensely colored and patterned hand-dyed and hand-painted fabrics, juxtaposed with a startling simplicity of form, characterize Sue Benner's work. Repetition and variation work to tame the riot of colors and patterns she uses, creating compelling imagery.

Dyeing and painting fabrics

I dye and paint many of the fabrics I use. For a large project or a new series, I will often create new fabrics especially for that purpose. I'll start with a few ideas, marks, or motifs in various colors, and see what happens. I always make many more fabrics than I will use. Other times I will dye and paint with no fixed use in mind. I'll later use these fabrics as my series work pulls them in. A particularly strong fabric can inspire a new direction in my work.

Another part of my studio practice is collecting and reusing found fabrics. Rescuing unloved textiles and thrift shopping are a great source of amusement for me.

Circles and lines

I know where the circle began for me, as the shape of a biological cell. Of course, not all cells are circular—many, maybe most, are not. But as a symbol of a cell, this works for me, and more specifically a dot within a circle representing a nucleus surrounded by

cytoplasm and a cell membrane. These are units that I can stack, assemble, and scatter in interesting ways providing possibilities for order and disorder. Circles are also polka dots, which make me happy to look at. Over time the circle has progressed to stand for other ideas: flowers, berries, atoms, molecules, ribosomes, seeds, eggs, etc.

At some point I deliberately began experimenting with lines in my work, or rather thin strips of fabric collaged to the surface. I could create direction and energy that way, and then I developed the use of bias strips to make the lines even more expressive. I now work with lines abstractly and figuratively as prairie grasses, but it doesn't really matter what they are. I am more intrigued by their directionality, overlap, and complexity.

OPPOSITE *Nest III*. 2002. 62" × 77".
Dyed and painted silk, cotton, and found fabrics. Fused collage, monoprinted, machine quilted. | Photo: John G. Lanning.

ABOVE *Wearing Plaid 2*. 2011. 57" × 57".
Dyed and painted silk, cotton, and found fabrics. Fused collage, machine quilted.

LEFT *Body Parts*. 2007. 81" × 61".
Dyed and painted silk, cotton, and found fabrics. Fused collage, monoprinted, machine quilted. | Photo: Eric Neilsen Photography.

Fascination with plaid

I like the structure of woven fabric, and I have been fascinated by plaids since I was a child. My mom made a lot of my clothes, and then I learned to sew as well. In Wisconsin, where I grew up, we often worked with a lot of wool and a lot of plaid. There was much instruction and discussion of even and uneven plaids, matching them at seams and across the entire garment. I looked at them intensely. In fact, I still like to wear plaid skirts. So some of my fascination with plaid is nostalgia.

I also like what happens when you look through a grid, when it's expanded and you can see what is behind it. Metal mesh and chain link fences are something I photograph all the time. They form a scrim for the scene behind. Instant units, instant quilt!

Need that buzzy feeling

I hate almost every piece at some point. Really hate it. But, then I get this buzzy feeling that it's going better and then I think it might *not* be the worst piece of you-know-what that I have ever seen. Then I finish it.

If something is not working or I am stuck, I let it sit up on the wall, on the table, on the floor, or in a box (if it is really bothering me) until I get an idea. Sometimes I finish pieces that I am not so sure about on one level, but realize on another that something is going on that I don't understand yet. I know that it is important for my process and development as an artist to continue working, even though I am uncomfortable. Once in a while, when a piece is really not working or subpar, I will take a huge chance of ruining it completely and print or paint over it.

Being uncertain about my work can be a transformational experience.

Cellular Structure III. 2006. 72" × 45".
Dyed and painted silk, cotton and found fabrics. Fused collage, monoprinted, machine quilted.
Photo: Eric Neilsen Photography.

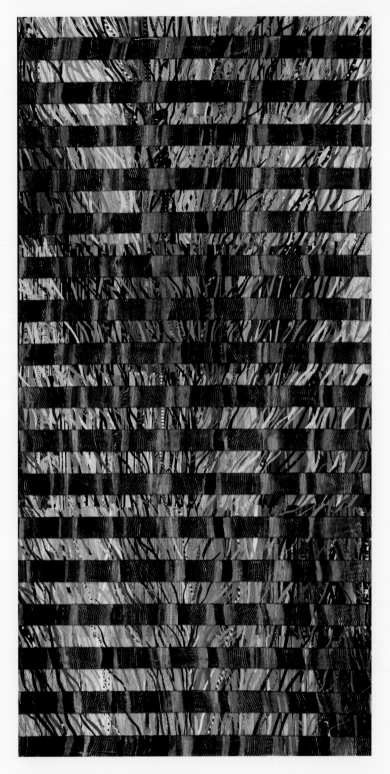

ABOVE *Tallgrass II*. 2015. 82" × 41".
Dyed and painted silk, cotton and found fabrics. Fused collage,
monoprinted, machine quilted.

LEFT *Walking through Time II: Gold on Gold.* 2006.
88" × 29". Dyed and painted silk, cotton and found fabrics.
Fused collage, monoprinted, machine quilted.
Photo: Eric Neilsen Photography.

197

Kent Williams

Madison, Wisconsin, USA

Changing hues play against the regularity of pieced bars to create a powerful visual tension in Kent Williams's work. Light and shadow seem to be woven together causing patterns to coalesce and disperse across the surface. Subtle color shifts in congruent forms create a patterned rhythm of mesmerizing movement.

Being a critic

Earlier careers in journalism as both an art critic and a movie critic led indirectly to my quilting interests. Critics have to be able to explain why they do or don't like something. And if you do that long enough, you start to develop an aesthetic—a set of principles that, although you're prepared to violate them at a moment's notice, nevertheless guide you toward what you think art is, not to mention what it could and should be. So, when I started quilting about fifteen years ago, I already had a pretty solid foundation to draw on. More importantly, I had a set of ideas that I wanted to explore.

That I chose to explore them through the medium of quilting was somewhat happenstance. I'd always loved quilts, in that pre-thought kind of way that I suspect most quilters can relate to. But when I started, I was just looking for something to snuggle under. Almost immediately, though, I was hooked. Making those first couple of quilts unleashed a latent design instinct that had been channeled into things like choosing the perfect rug to go with that brown leather couch. The art instinct kicked in, too.

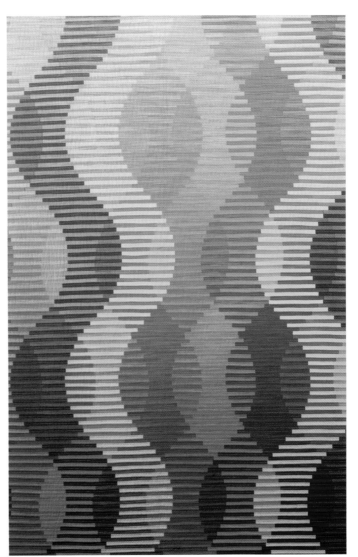

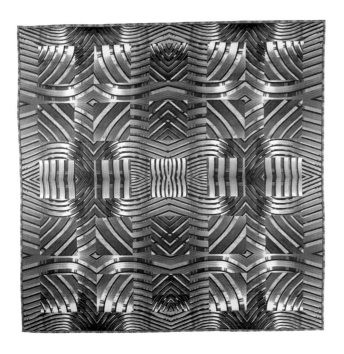

OPPOSITE *Blue Ribbon*. 2009. 54" × 54".
Cotton. Machine pieced and quilted. | Photo: Eric Tadsen.

ABOVE *Heavy Metal*. 2015. 48" × 48".
Digitally printed cotton sateen. Machine quilted.

RIGHT *Sine Me Up*. 2009. 82" × 62".
Cotton. Machine pieced and quilted. | Photo: Eric Tadsen.

Traditions

I like honoring the quilting traditions. For a long time, I used only commercial fabrics, partly because of the limitations they imposed, but mostly because that's what quilters have done for hundreds of years. I've also done a lot of piecing, which seems relatively rare these days, but if I hadn't pieced my quilts, I would have probably drifted off to another medium a long time ago. Which leads to my third refusal to break with the past: I use pattern. I'm mesmerized by pattern. I see it everywhere and have come to believe that it's the basis of everything we know about the world.

Algorithm-like operations

Spiral-based designs, like *Sine Me Up* and *Googie-Woogie*, make use of the Fibonacci sequence, a series of numbers each of which is derived by adding together the two previous numbers in the series. And what I like about the Fibonacci sequence is that it allows me to delineate a graceful curve while using straight-line fabric pieces, which are of course much easier to sew.

I like to send sets of fabrics past one another to form patterns that owe something to both choice and chance. As an example, I will take one gradient fabric, slice it into small rectangular shapes, then alternate those rectangular shapes with similar ones from a separate gradient fabric. This sets up a constantly evolving color interaction while holding on to the consistency of the underlying gradient fabrics. I'm a total sucker for pattern, but it has to be a pattern that's constantly changing. Pattern that doesn't change is mere wallpaper.

Quilts and computers

My interest in deriving content from computers, which I see as the most powerful force in today's visual culture, wound up pushing me temporarily out of quilting altogether. Faced with what I regarded as the limitations of the quilt medium—the number of individual fabric pieces that can be squeezed

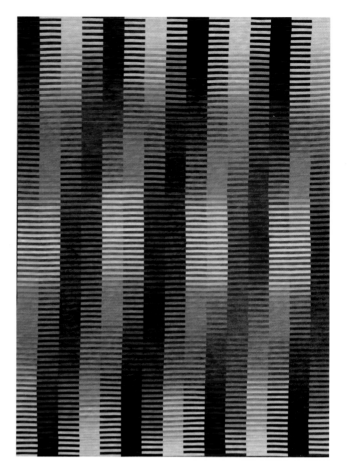

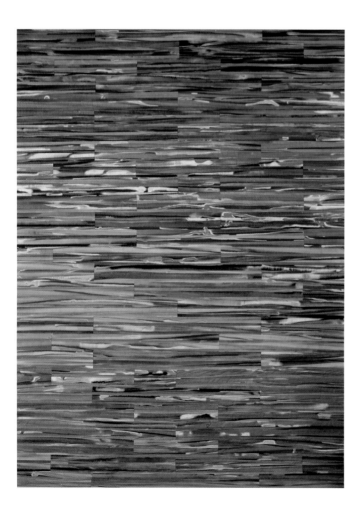

into a single quilt, for instance—I looked around for a medium that might accommodate my desire to evoke the intricate complexity of the digital age. That turned out to be digital art. For a couple of years now, I've been using image-processing applications to create works that I then have printed on archival-quality paper. Much of it is what I would call quilt-like, except it doesn't take me near as long to complete.

However, there was something about quilting that kept calling me, and I started to feel the juices stirring again. In the last year, I've started designing pieces on the computer, then having them printed out on fabric. This is a whole new direction for me, and I'm very excited about bringing some of the lessons I've learned from digital art to my quilting.

ABOVE *Light-Emitting Fabric*. 2009. 82" × 59". Cotton. Machine pieced and quilted. | Photo: Eric Tadsen.

LEFT *Lake Mendota*. 2009. 80" × 60". Cotton. Machine pieced and quilted. | Photo: Eric Tadsen.

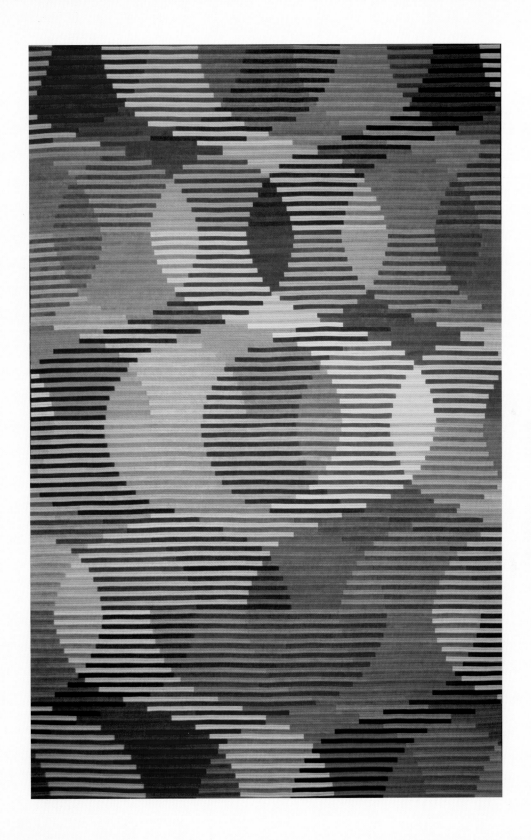

Art = Beautiful + Interesting

I suspect that this formula wouldn't hold up to a lot of scrutiny, but the point I am trying to make is that having created a pretty object isn't enough. There has to be an idea—ideally one that can't quite be put into words—behind the pretty object for it to qualify as art. I like a pretty object as much as the next person; it just needs to say something, hopefully something that hasn't been said in quite that way before.

Googie-Woogie. 2010. 78" × 50". Cotton. Machine pieced and quilted. Photo: Eric Tadsen.

Willy Doreleijers

Dordrecht, the Netherlands

Dynamic use of line defines much of Willy Doreleijers's work. Lines crisscross, emerge and disappear, expand and fade. While some of her pieces are very colorful, it is Doreleijers's use of line that creates tremendous energy in her art. She also delights in playing games with the viewers—now you see the image; now you don't—as shapes advance and recede from the picture plane.

Seamstress

I have always loved textiles. It was actually my grandmother who first got me interested in knitting and sewing. After years of making things in my free time, I decided to join an evening course in costume design. I learned all the skills for pattern drawing and designing clothes, as well as embroidery techniques. But somehow this still did not satisfy my abiding interest in textiles.

Skills are useful for making textile work, but they are not the most important thing. The most important goal that I have for making good work is the ability to express my ideas in a visual way.

Painting classes

I had several years of personal guidance from a textile artist who also was a teacher at the Art Academy in Maastricht. Some years after his death I decided to take coaching sessions from a painter who also is an art teacher at the Art Academy in Haarlem. Topics have included portraying feelings and impressions; looking at and understanding other forms of art; interpreting art; what position art has in society, etc. This has definitely shaped the works I currently make. The development and evolution of art is continuous and has no end.

OPPOSITE *Neurotic City*. 2012. 50" × 48".
Cotton, polyester organza. Batik, transfer dyed, stenciled, machine stitched.
Photo: Herman Lengton.

Roombeek. 2008. 59" × 35".
Cotton, high-tech fabrics from Ten Cate, Angelina film. Dyed, stenciled, appliquéd, machine stitched. | Photo: Herman Lengton.

Where ideas come from

I find ideas everywhere. I can be sitting on a terrace and notice how the light of the sun plays with the passersby. My husband designed a new building in the monumental center of the city, and its lines are exciting to me. I suddenly noticed how the street where we live contains interesting repeating patterns. I try to capture what I've seen in photos, and then use them as the basis for creating a new design.

Screen prints

I used to draw out my designs with pencil and paper. Now I work digitally. The result is immediately visible but also easy to change. I like how screen prints allow me to make parts transparent and add layers that create depth. Through experimentation in combining the layers in various ways, new possibilities arise. All this ultimately results in a design that works for me. The design is then printed out at full size on paper and becomes my pattern. Shape and color are ninety-five percent set at this stage and implementation in textiles can progress.

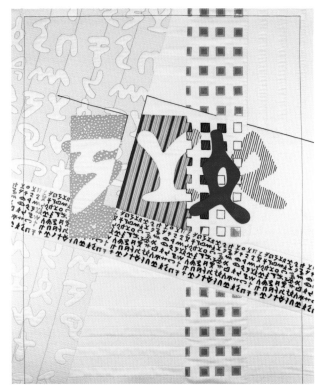

Lines and color

I like graphics. The game of lines and colors is an important factor in my work. The composition ultimately determines which lines and colors go together or whether an image will be built up individually. A good example of this is *Dutch Color*. The mill is shown in two colors and an image of the mill in the background gives the same lines. The viewer is asked to look closely to discover the additional image.

Urban inspiration

Neurotic City is a picture of the street where I live. The question I asked myself was: Should my depiction of the city be closer to reality or fiction? The answer was . . . both! I created a street view of a typical Dutch street where historic facades are mixed with new contemporary elements. For us, as humans, we are constantly faced with changing fashion trends and technology images, and we find that perfectly acceptable. But how does the city experience itself? The city continues to innovate and therefore has eternal youth. Past and present are clearly reflected in the facades. Yet in the psyche of the city there is conflict about how to accommodate these changes. This manifests itself in a tilted structure with the environment incomprehensible, a desperate, insecure, and theatrical representation of reality. That's why I titled it *Neurotic City*.

OPPOSITE

ABOVE *Found Memory*. 2014. 33" × 46".
Cotton, polyester organza. Batik, transfer dyed, machine stitched. | Photo: Herman Lengton.

LEFT *Fenische Eye-Path*. 2010. 39" × 31".
Cotton. Batik, screenprinted, dyed, appliquéd, machine stitched. | Photo: Herman Lengton.

RIGHT *Fenische E-reader*. 2010. 39" × 31".
Cotton. Batik, screenprinted, dyed, appliquéd, machine stitched. | Photo: Herman Lengton.

Dutch Colors. 2009. 47" × 39".
Cotton. Batik, machine stitched.
Photo: Herman Lengton.

Phoenician Letters

With my series *Phoenician Letters (Fenische)*, I was inspired by the Phoenician script and the inhabitants of Phoenicia. In ancient times, Phoenicia was an important region on the east coast of the Mediterranean Sea. In addition to their navigational skills, the Phoenicians also acquired great wealth as suppliers of the much-coveted purplish-red dye for textiles.

The Phoenician script, the oldest alphabet that is known, was fundamental to the development of the Hebrew, Greek, Latin, and Arabic scripts. In our electronic age we consider the Phoenician signs as a very ancient and frozen message from a long-ago past. With my art pieces I am referring to contemporary communication possibilities, such as e-mail, iPads, e-readers and apps. Texts are represented in a very different way from how the Phoenicians wrote in 800 BCE, but both have a similar goal of conveying a message. I hope that my art achieves that goal as well.

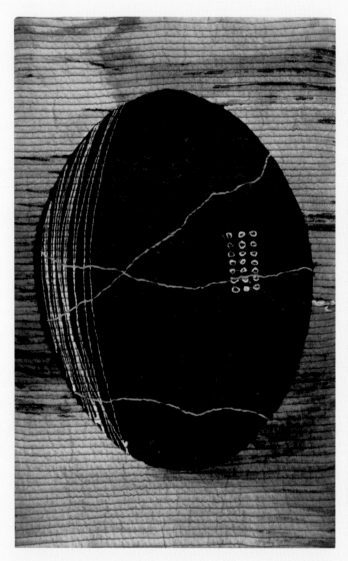

Karen Rips

Thousand Oaks, California, USA

Furrows of rippling fabric surround lines of quilting in Karen Rips's artwork. Amorphous shapes appear and disappear from the discharged fabrics as couched lines meander and swirl across the surface. Recent work, inspired by medical imaging such as X-rays and MRIs, creates poignant portraits of the human condition.

Discovering quilt art

As a child I was never really either encouraged or discouraged from making art. It was not part of my upbringing, so my only exposure was in grade school and frankly I had little interest in art. I went to school for nursing and started a career in a neonatal unit at our hospital.

My first exposure to art quilts came in the early 1990s after we had moved to Thousand Oaks, California, when I discovered Eileen Albers's store The Quilters' Studio. At that time, Eileen offered classes, supplies, and studio space for everything art quilt related. As the name implies, The Quilters' Studio was more than a fabric store: it was a place where people gathered to make art. I began to see the possibilities of using textiles in many different ways and to view my sewing room as a studio or art space.

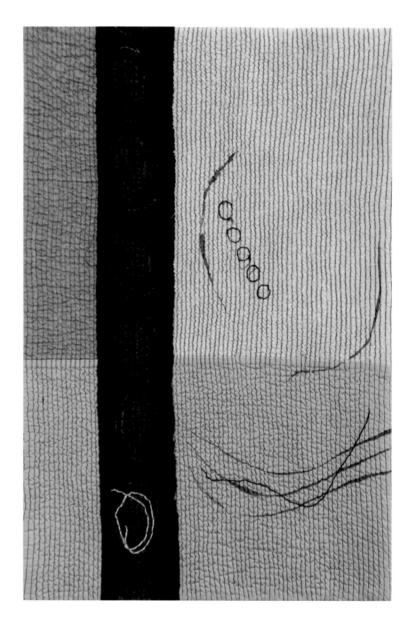

OPPOSITE

LEFT *Realization*. 2014. 51" × 35".
Cotton, paint. Soy waxed, discharged, painted, machine and hand stitched. | Photo: Ted Rips.

RIGHT *Consciousness*. 2013. 17" × 11".
Cotton, paint. Soy waxed, discharged, painted, machine and hand stitched. | Photo: Ted Rips.

ABOVE *Meditation*. 2012. 60" × 24".
Cotton. Soy waxed, discharged, machine and hand stitched. | Photo: Ted Rips.

RIGHT Karen Rips. *MM2*. 2013. 24" × 16".
Cotton. Dyed, soy waxed, discharged, overdyed, machine and hand stitched. | Photo: Ted Rips.

Texture through felting

I create a heavily textured surface in my pieces by quilting over wool batting and then felting the whole piece, which causes the wool batting to shrink and creates wonderful texture in the surface. Quilting over wool batting and then felting is not original to me. I first learned of this technique from a book by C. June Barnes called *Stitching to Dye in Quilt Art: Colour, Texture and Distortion* (Batsford, 2009). I started experimenting with this method and have been using it pretty steadily since then.

In 2010, I created three pieces that I believe were pivotal to my development. They were my first studies using this technique and were the first pieces that I mounted on canvas. They were purely experimental pieces, but they worked. Looking back at my earlier work, I have always liked texture. This technique is ideal for producing the surface I want.

Image comes first

I usually start with an image, real or imagined. Sometimes I use pictures from vacations or photos of things that capture my attention. Sometimes they are images that are conjured up in my head. But for me the image comes first, not the color.

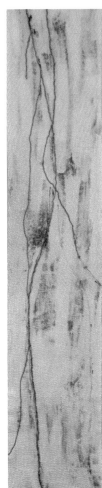

I used to work spontaneously, but now I tend to sketch out the lines I'm thinking about using before I commit to fabric. I'll make several quick sketches, trying not to be too specific. With some of my work, such as the two pieces about Alzheimer's, I plan it all out in my mind in advance of starting.

In my collaborative work with Paula Chung, I usually start with an MRI, X-ray, or some other form of medical imaging and try to get a sense of what I want to say about it. This can be difficult. For instance, when you see an image of a fetal ultrasound, the first thing that most people notice is the bean-like shape of the growing child. Since I work in the abstract, I try to capture and distill the image into lines and

ABOVE *The Journey.* 2014. 60" × 39".
Cotton. Dyed, soy waxed, discharged, overdyed, machine and hand stitched. | Photo: Ted Rips.

LEFT *Road Trip.* 2014. 70" × 46".
Cotton. Dyed, soy waxed, discharged, overdyed, machine and hand stitched. | Photo: Ted Rips.

Bundle of Sorrow. 2015. 84" × 48" × 24". Nylon cord, rusted sheet metal, fishing line, cheesecloth, tea bags, encaustic wax, paper. Encaustic, gesso coating, rusted, hand stitched. | Photo: Ted Rips.

shapes, which swoop and curve, sometimes connecting and sometimes not. *The Journey* is part of this series.

Another example is based on the images I saw of someone's brain who had Alzheimer's, which showed the build-up of plaque and the severe empty areas in the brain. *Road Trip* is a response to how this brain image, rather than being made up of serene curving shapes, created a feeling that the brain was stark, straight, and cut up, while at the same time trying desperately to remain organized.

Importance of collaboration

Thinking about my artistic path, I realize I have made some of my best work in collaborations. That could be because I need someone else to raise the bar or perhaps I feel the need to honor the commitment that comes with a partnership. My most recent collaboration, *A View Within*, started when Paula Chung, who is a member of my local critique group, showed me her art quilt where she had interpreted an X-ray in stitch. I was blown away and asked if I could do something similar. My background in nursing very much influenced me in pursuing this.

After four years I am still excited about this collaboration and what we are doing, because we continually push each other to try new things even if they don't always work out. We both respect each other's work enough that we can be comfortable together as a collaboration and as individuals and have both shown separately at various venues. Because we are very open with each other on what we want to do as individuals and together as a partnership, there are no drawbacks for me in this process.

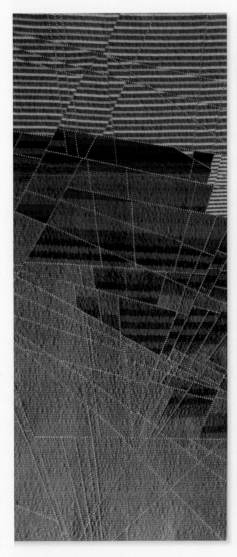

Kathleen Loomis

Louisville, Kentucky, USA

"Craze" means to produce a network of fine cracks on a surface. And it perfectly describes the effect that Kathleen Loomis creates in her art. Dedication to the art of machine piecing has led to increasingly complex designs. The interplay of fine intersecting lines and subtle color variation forms a network that teases the eye and puzzles the mind.

Lines

When I started working with fine lines, I had two different techniques, which I describe as large-to-small and small-to-large. Large-to-small is starting with a large piece of fabric, cutting it apart, sewing it back together with a line in between, then repeating and repeating and repeating. Small-to-large is the opposite, starting with small pieces of fabric, stitching them together into long strips or modules with lines in between, then building the modules into larger and larger expanses. My *Fault Lines* series started as pure large-to-small, while my *Crazed* series was small-to-large.

But after making several *Fault Lines* quilts, I found there wasn't that much left to explore in the large-to-small approach. I never want to make the same quilt over again, merely changing the colors; instead I always want to incorporate some new element. So what happened with the large-to-small approach is that it got hybridized: I use large-to-small techniques to make modules, and then build the modules into full quilts. The combination of pure bisecting lines and modular construction allows me to make very complex networks, which is my intent and pleasure.

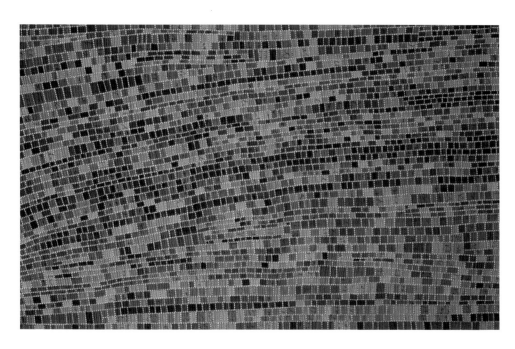

OPPOSITE *Entropy*. 2014. 86" × 71". Cotton. Machine pieced and quilted. Photo: George Plager.

———

ABOVE *Crazed 9: Blue State Blues*. 2010. 41" × 66". Cotton. Machine pieced and quilted, handwriting. Photo: George Plager.

RIGHT *Crazed 16: Suburban Dream*. 2012. 55" × 81". Cotton. Machine pieced and quilted. Photo: George Plager.

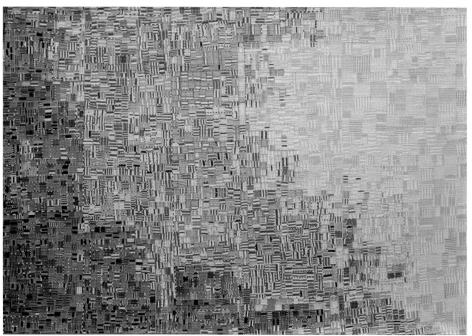

Big Ice. 2012. 78" × 32".
Cotton. Machine pieced and quilted.
Photo: George Plager.

Fault Lines 3. 2010. 78" × 75".
Cotton. Machine pieced and quilted.
Photo: George Plager.

Designs do not start visually

I do some of my best thinking about art when I can't sleep in the middle of the night. Probably my most important insight is that I really do not think about my art visually, at least in the initial creative stages. When developing a new idea, it happens in sentences, not in pictures. I never sketch when starting a new quilt; instead I have a list of things that I want to accomplish—a color palette, a technique, a density of line, and probably several other elements. I have a verbal description, often in considerable detail, but I don't know what it's going to look like until I make it.

I look on my fine lines as a metaphor for the fragile bonds that hold our society, our environment, and our infrastructure together. Even though the quilts are abstract, they are all about something, and I have given them all specific titles that refer to some aspect of this interconnected jeopardy. *Fault Lines* alludes to unstable earth formations that could slip at any moment. My *Crazed* series is about things that we cannot control or that we have allowed to get out of control—for instance, war, pollution, weather, politics, and natural disasters.

When I started sewing striped fabrics together to make *Crazed 8*, I saw them as a whole lot of little guys wearing stripes, behind bars. We have allowed our use of prisons to get entirely out of control, so *Incarceration* was a perfect metaphorical fit for this piece.

Fabrics talk to me

I'm not a woo-woo kind of person, but I believe that if I put some fabric up on the design wall where I can see it, it will talk to me. Sometimes I'll pin fabrics up before I even start cutting and piecing to figure out what I'm going to do with them. More

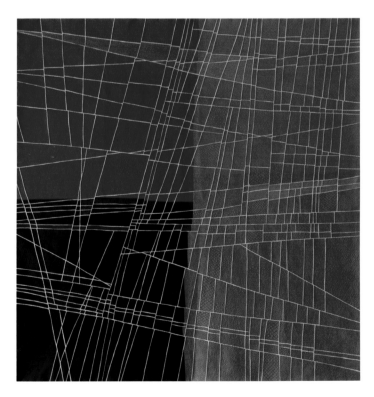

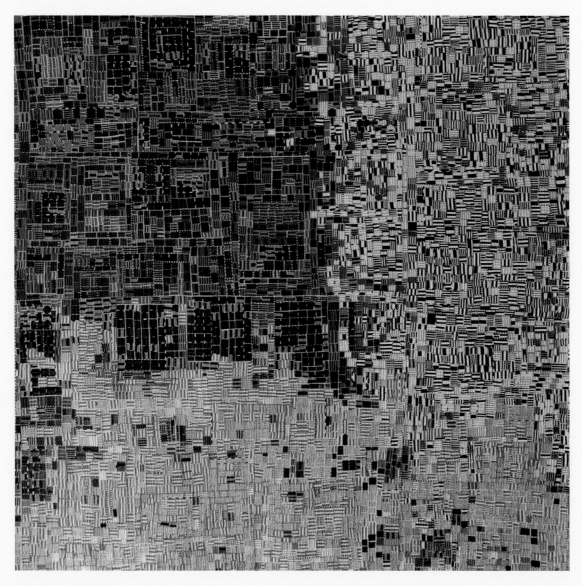

Crazed 8: Incarceration. 2010. 82" × 79".
Cotton. Machine pieced and quilted. | Photo: George Plager.

frequently, I'll piece some modules and put them up and see what they say, whether they play well with their neighbors, and whether they want to keep going.

I know when things are going well because I am impelled to keep on sewing. When I start getting antsy and find myself doing the laundry or fixing dinner instead of sewing, I know that I need to take a break. If it's a simple problem that needs to be solved I'll pin things on the design wall and wait for them to reveal what they need while I work on something else, or if all else fails, clean the studio.

Fine art of machine piecing

I think that machine piecing is an endangered art for some very good reasons. It's much faster to get an image on your quilt with surface design, fusing, or raw edge appliqué than it is with piecing, and it's easier to achieve precisely what you want. Piecing adds the element of the seam allowance—the pieces you cut from the fabric aren't exactly what you will end up with in the finished quilt—that you have to mentally incorporate into your planning and execution, especially if you work improvisationally rather than with templates, and that makes it more difficult. I love the hard edge of the seam where two fabrics meet.

I think the number of people who are working with elaborate piecing—that is, piecing using a bazillion seams and a fair amount of obsessive construction—is getting smaller all the time. Because I happen to be good at this skill, and I enjoy the zen of sitting at the sewing machine, I feel an almost moral obligation to keep doing it, to help keep this skill alive, and keep this art form in the public eye. I have therefore made a conscious decision that I want my reputation as a quiltmaker to be as a fine machine piecer.

Judy Rush
Bexley, Ohio, USA

Richly layered fabrics combine with clusters of scattered, stitched marks to create deeply personal messages in Judy Rush's work. Seeing fabric as the "fundamental feminine transfer material," the energy vibrations coming from each piece affect how she works. With compositions based on designs generated through the use of sacred geometry, her art is a way to explore her relationships with family and society.

Surface design

I just love to meander through all the different options available for surface design. I love that we can do so many fabulous modifications to the surface with everyday items we buy at the grocery store. Some of my go-to traditional surface design techniques are block printing, resist, discharge, and screen printing.

I print and reprint over everything. I usually start out with an idea of where I want to go, but very quickly I lose track of that process and find myself involved in a different direction. I often use a soy wax resist to begin, then layer prints over top of that. When the wax and print paste is removed, the design is no longer what I expected. I may discharge or re-dye or use the fabric as I printed it the first time. The fabric I use the most of (silk gauze) is very expensive. I may continue to use a fabric for years, so that I use every scrap. I discharge and re-dye pieces of it, until it is all used up.

Portraits

I was raised as a typical 1960s and '70s type girl. Any job outside the home always took second place to the work inside the home. With that training, I learned how to raise children: how they need structure and constant safety checks, how to keep them fed and clean, and most of all how to enjoy them. I had a great time with my kids. I loved every minute growing with them . . . then they grew up, and I was out of tools.

To remedy that I first had to imagine a relationship with my children as adults. Since I did not have anything to use as strategies and since my children are not cookie cutter human beings, I had to make up my own approach. Working on this series around them has helped me to identify what that relationship could look like. It has given me the opportunity to experience new options, and in lots of ways, it has brought a new clarity.

OPPOSITE *Portrait of the Middle Child 1*. 2013. 29" × 37".
Silk, cotton, silk and rayon velvet, paper, Swedish lace, Swedish nursing uniform. Devoré, laminated, printed, silk screened, hand stitched and embroidered.

Waking Up. 2013. 36" × 58".
Silk, cotton, silk and rayon velvet, paper, Swedish lace, Swedish nursing uniform. Devoré, laminated, printed, silk screened, hand stitched and embroidered.

Sacred geometry

I have been using sacred geometry to explore the faces of my adult children. To that end, I cover every line of a photo of their faces with a nautilus spiral I call the Golden Spiral. The Golden Spiral is a geometric pattern generated from a mathematical sequence called the Fibonacci series. The only rule in doing this mapping is that I must maintain the relational proportions of the shape. It is, after all, the relationships to each other that create balance. If I change the relationship, I change the balance.

I am finished when I can redraw the image using only the lines generated from the spirals. I use the information of the lines to generate a composition. I am interested in how the composition reflects the relationship between me and my subject, but also in how the composition moves the eye around the page.

My Own Politics. 2008. 35" × 43".
Hand-dyed silk, cotton. Laminated, printed, silk screened, hand stitched and embroidered.

Flight. 2015. 36" × 40".
Hand-dyed and -printed silks, rayon, cotton, paper. Hand stitched and embroidered.

Stitching squares

Stitching squares is another way to explore my relationships. There were long periods of time when I felt like I had very few choices in my life. The squares are representations of windows, or doors, or boundaries of some kind. Trying to look out, trying to see in, trying to get out, stay in, stay in line. Keeping the space ordered and easy in some manner. Finding a path, finding safe passage.

At the same time, I think the squares may be more meditative at this point than mysterious. It is easy to sew in a straight line. I can sew in the opposite direction in a straight line and make squares. I don't have to concentrate. I can sew and enjoy the act of stitching.

Expression

My work is about expression. It is about learning to live my life in the way I want to live it. There are many beliefs and baggage I carry into my adult life. The work has become about learning to strip all that away. Exploring my resistance to all things.

If a piece of work can be judged as going well, not going well, then there is resistance; and resistance inhibits growth. I am always learning from my experiences. My art must mirror my life. They are one in the same; it is how I operate in the world.

ABOVE *Portrait of the Youngest Girl 1*. 2010. 39" × 25".
Hand-dyed silk, cotton, silk and rayon velvet. Devoré, laminated, printed, silk screened, hand stitched and embroidered.

LEFT *Portrait of the Youngest Girl 2*. 2010. 31" × 51".
Hand-dyed silk, cotton, silk and rayon velvet, audio tape. Devoré, laminated, printed, silk screened, hand stitched and embroidered.

Toot Reid

Tacoma, Washington, USA

Monumental size, vibrant color, and mysterious symbols all characterize Toot Reid's art. Each piece is a record of how her emotions reacted with the cloth over a period of weeks and months. The stitched markings are an intuitive response to the process: sometimes the stitching is in contrast to the fabrics; sometimes it blends in. Always the power of the artist's vision comes through.

OPPOSITE *September 28, 2010 – March 8, 2011.*
2011. 63" × 98".
Cotton, silk and metal fabric. Machine pieced,
stitched, and appliquéd, hand quilted.
Photo: Ken Wagner.

Thirteen. 2002. 94" × 75".
Cotton. Machine pieced, stitched, and appliquéd,
hand quilted. | Photo: Ken Wagner.

Dates as titles

My sister was diagnosed with cancer in 2005. At that time I was
working on large, single pieces that could take from six to eight
months to complete. As I was helping my sister and dealing with my
own emotions, I realized that six months was too long to work on one
piece. I needed to put down my feelings more quickly.

I came up with the idea of the pieces being my height and using
the dates as a way of documenting my life. The dates are beginnings
and endings, because I didn't want one piece to go on and on. The end
date is whenever I feel I am done. I don't plan an end date. The end is
whenever it is right.

219

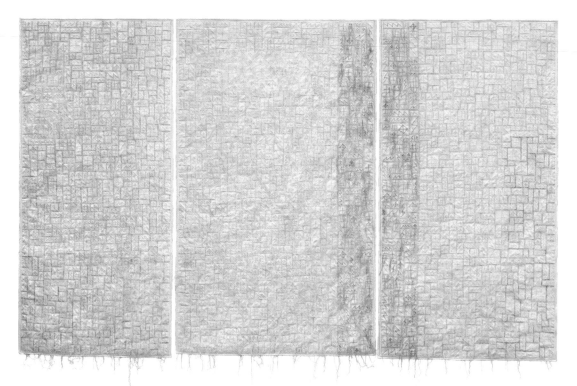

Design by intuition

I do not make sketches. I look at my fabric, check in
with how I'm feeling and start pulling out pieces that
feel right. I always have more at the beginning than I
end up using. Then I eliminate or add. I make a few sections and sew the thread on top to see if the fabric and
thread work. After I decide that, I spend days making
pieces or "tiles." I hand cut all the small pieces. There
are usually about six or seven different sizes and anywhere from six to nine different colors of fabric.

 I make all the tile pieces, sew the top threads on,
and then I sit down on a large piece of backing fabric, the canvas. I begin at the top left hand corner, and
I place the tile pieces. I lay out about ten to fifteen
pieces at a time, pin them, and then take the whole
construction to the sewing machine and sew the pieces down. Then I take it back to the floor and place the
next group. Sometimes I know I'm going to change colors partway through and I work to wherever I feel that
a break is right and then change. Sometimes I change
the background fabric, so the change comes from the
back color and not the front. Again, this is all from feel,
with no sketching or preconceived plan.

ABOVE *August 5, 2008 – March 28, 2009. 2009. 63" × 103".*
Cotton. Machine pieced, stitched, and appliquéd, hand quilted.
Photo: Ken Wagner.

RIGHT *October 1, 2012 – October 30, 2012. 63" × 39".*
Cotton. Machine pieced, stitched, and appliquéd, hand quilted.
Photo: Dane Meyer.

Importance of the threads

Fabric doesn't have any depth; what makes depth is shadow. So the space between the small sections is important. Sewing down the tile pieces to the background fabric and having batting makes for some shadowing, some depth. Raising thread to the same level of importance as the fabrics was a big breakthrough for me. I now let all the loose threads accumulate and hang. And the threads create depth. One needs to look through the threads to the pieces and colors behind. The threads have become a critical design component.

Passage of time

I think some of working large has to do with the fact that I was the shortest person in my family and the youngest, so it is a way to be noticed. Also, I read something artist Barnett Newman said about size: that he wanted his work to be walked through. He meant that the piece is so large that you can walk beside it and be in it as time passes.

What I want viewers to understand about the dates in my titles is the passage of time. There is a start date, but I never know what the end date will be or how many panels there will be. I put down an end date for each piece, but I think of the next piece I start as being a continuation of the previous conversation I was having with the work.

November 2, 2012 – February 4, 2013. 2013. 63" × 95". Cotton. Machine pieced, stitched, and appliquéd, hand quilted. Photo: Dane Meyer.

Featured Artists

Gallery Artists